BNI One Bite at a Time

By David Wimblett

Foreword by
Dr. Ivan Misner

Book design by
Richard Tomlin – The Fusion Effect

First Published 2011 by
DJW Business Systems Limited – London

Thank You

To my Mum and Dad who always believed
in me and to whom I owe so much.

Foreword

BNI's mission is to help their members increase business through a structured, positive and professional word-of-mouth programme that enables them to develop long-term, meaningful relationships with quality business professionals. Point blank, membership in BNI is an opportunity to turn your time and commitment into a lot of money for yourself and your fellow members. So how, as a BNI member, do you take full advantage of this opportunity and maximize the results from your participation and efforts? Reading this book is a great place to start.

Based on seven years of experience as a BNI member who has reaped great rewards as a result of participating in weekly BNI meetings, David Wimblett has compiled this invaluable, easy-to-read handbook on how to approach BNI membership for truly powerful results. Filled with practical and fresh nuggets of wisdom, tips, ideas, and strategies that are essential for BNI members worldwide in maximizing their return on investment from BNI membership, this book should be in every BNI member's library as a go-to informational resource and it is especially essential for those filling the role of Education Coordinator in their BNI chapter.

Whether you are brand new to BNI or you have been in BNI for years, utilizing the simple strategies outlined within these pages will not only ensure that you get the absolute most out of every aspect of BNI membership, it will show you how weekly life in BNI can be amazingly rewarding and fun. If you've ever struggled with how to come to terms with the time commitment associated with weekly meetings, adhering to the structured networking environment of BNI, or the idea of investing in your fellow members by adopting the Givers Gain® philosophy, look no further than this book. David truly understands what BNI is all about and he explains in crystal-clear terms how to approach BNI proactively by taking small bites, so to speak, so you will never bite off more than you can chew while always making the most of the opportunities BNI membership presents.

Ivan Misner, NY Times Bestselling Author and Founder of BNI and Referral Institute

Who is
David Wimblett?

Tuesday 18th January 2011, BNI Director training in Reading. In the room are over one hundred BNI Directors: Regional Directors, Assistant Directors, Area Directors, Executive Directors and National Directors.

A question has been asked about the best places to find Education Slots. The answers have included Dr. Ivan Misner's books, the director part of the BNI web site and Success-Net. Another hand goes up and the person says, *"Another great resource is David Wimblett's blog."* (I didn't see who it was, but if you are reading this – thank you!)

During the break directors handed me their business cards and ask if they can be added to the distribution list for my blog.

So, who am I?

Currently I am a business mentor and trainer (and blogger). I started my first business at the age of 21 and over the following thirty years have tried and experienced most things that business can throw at you. In 2003 I joined BNI, becoming a Regional Director in 2006.

During all of this time, other than really enjoying what I was doing, the one thing that stood out for me was that people asked me for advice on business matters: how would I cope with a particular problem, or even success? A soon-to-be Chapter Director asked if I could tell him everything I knew about BNI. I said no, not really, but instead started to write this blog.

BNI blog: My BNI Day:
http://bnigivers.blogspot.com
Business blog:
http://davidsbetterbusiness-
blog.wordpress.com/
7 Training:
http://www.7training.co.uk

In 2010 I sold my share of Imperial Printers to my partner, so that I could concentrate on what I am now truly passionate about: helping business owners to have even more success. I think this goes back to my first few years in business, where, if it had not been for two great people, I might have failed, but also my love of seeing people in business have both fun and the success they ought to have.

I hope you enjoy my book and that it helps, in some way, to make your time in BNI both more fun and a great deal more profitable.

Why a BNI Blog?

3/2/08

Well it's simple really. I've been in BNI for some time now, have held every position in a chapter, attended numerous training sessions, been to every workshop, visited different chapters, subbed at other chapters, attended Awards Dinners, Member Days, forums and all manner of social events.

During this time I have talked to a great many people from Dr. Ivan Misner to Frank J. De Raffele Jr., to Mr and Mrs Lawson, to Area Directors, Regional Directors, Leadership Teams, Committee Members and members. And from every single one learned something useful. On top of that I have developed my own ideas on things. So I have a head full of all this experience, some good, some bad, that is just sort of there!

I became an RD so that I could give something back and pass some experience on, and it was when I was talking to a soon-to-be Chapter Director that he said if only you could write all this stuff down for me. Easier said than done I said. Where would I start?

So this is for him. A collection of thoughts, as they come to me, that may help anyone in BNI. They are my thoughts and have not been okayed by BNI, so please do not assume that what I say is backed by BNI. I will say, however, that everything I say I hope will help you get more out of BNI and understand what a great business BNI is.

For my friend Gareth Miller that soon-to-be Chapter Director

What type are you?

3/2/08

There are all kinds of people in BNI, from those that 'get it' the moment they walk into their very first meeting, all the way through to those, who although they join, never really discover what BNI is all about and so never really get the true value out of their membership.

And, it starts with what type of member you are. Do you really believe in the philosophy of 'Givers Gain' and will you give BNI the benefit of the doubt that they may have just got things right after 22 years?

Now I'm not saying that everything about BNI is correct, and I doubt that they would either, as things are changing all the time and can be developed. But I think you need to understand how and why things work before you try changing them, or just not doing them.

I was having a coffee with a member a while ago, during a break in training, and he was saying that he almost didn't renew for his second year, but luckily for him he had. During his first year of membership he had turned up for meetings and hoped to get some referrals, and sadly didn't get many, but just enough to put pen to his renewal. Then something happened to change his viewpoint (he had no idea what), but suddenly he was going to meetings thinking 'I've got referrals to give today'. And guess what? He has received far more back!

I did an education slot once entitled 'Non-Givers Lose', as I really believe that although givers really do gain, non-givers lose out more. But more about that later.

How about trying an experiment? For the next month, try 'giving' in every way you can, without any thought of a return and see what happens. You may just be surprised at the results.

Finding visitors is a pain!

6/2/08

Some BNI members, and I guess some of you may be the same, think finding visitors to come to their BNI chapter is a pain.

But it doesn't have to be that way!

Why? Because I think that every visitor I bring along to my chapter could become my next client. And how good would it be to meet with a client every week over breakfast and build a really strong relationship with them?

How many of your customers are happy to see you every week for a couple of hours? No pressure on either side to make or resist a sale and what's the chance of you not knowing what they are buying or planning?

My company's bank manager is in my chapter. Do you know how good it is to see your bank manager every week? The bank is even buying from me now. The marketing company we use is also in my chapter, as is our solicitor. The list goes on and on.

So forget about BNI when inviting people and just think about your next customer or supplier. You will be surprised what a difference it makes.

I can't do that date!

9/2/08

Have you ever been at a meeting when the Treasurer is announcing the next six speakers and it goes something like this?

"Bob you're next week, Steve then it's you on the 15th, James 22nd, Clive 29th ...", but Clive cuts in and says he can't do the 29th. The Treasurer then asks Sally, but she's away, Jean is on a course and no-one else has their diary with them. So it ends up a mess and *"Oh well, I'll confirm next week"*, says the Treasurer.

Tell me: what does that say to any visitors? And, more important, what does it say about the Treasurer? Do they run their business that way? Would I refer to someone that disorganised?

And do you know the really silly thing? With just a little planning the Treasurer can look like the most efficient person on the planet.

How? Email. In fact, any communication before the meeting. If Clive had been asked before the meeting and then Sally and Jean, all the problem dates would have been sorted out and when the next six speakers were read out, they would have already been agreed. The meeting would have run more smoothly, saving time, and the Treasurer would have shown off their management skills.

8

So easy and so much better for the chapter and Treasurer alike. And the real big benefit? An increase in the chance of a referral for the Treasurer!

Nice blog. I agree with your comments about scheduling the speakers. That posting would make a good piece for SuccessNet. If you'd like, you should send it to our editor at bunny@customzines.com .

All the best.
Dr. Ivan Misner, Founder, BNI

Death and taxes: the only certainties!

10/2/08

Well if you are a BNI member, add another – the Substitute.

Substitutes seem to be a perennial problem amongst the majority of members and I've never worked out why, as the moment that you are inducted into your chapter you know that you will some day need a substitute.

I've heard members say among other things, *"The pressure of finding a sub..."*, *"I just don't know where to find one"*, and even, *"Can't BNI give us a list?"*.

I just can't understand why! A sub can be anyone: your partner, parent, friend, neighbour, work-mate, supplier, customer (who better to sing your praises?), golf partner, local shopkeeper.... The list is endless. After all, BNI is a networking organisation, so surely members must know someone?!

Then again, what about a visitor as a sub?

But if you still think finding a substitute is hard, how about trying my 'phone a friend' system. It's what I tell all the members I mentor.

New people to your chapter make the best subs, but if that really worries you then this is what I suggest.

Today phone some friends and make a list. You need three groups. Tell them you are in BNI and what we do. Tell them what a sub is and tell them that they get the chance to talk about their business (if they have one) and that they get a free breakfast as well. Then you need to find a couple of people that will sub for you with two weeks' notice, two that will sub for you with a week's notice and lastly two really good friends that will sub for you at 24 hours' notice.

All that pressure gone! When you then need a sub you just pick up the phone and make a call.

One last tip – a last resort. When other subs come to your chapter, collect their cards and put them in the back of your BNI folder. These are people you know will sub and if you really get stuck.... well, it's better than ABSENT against your name. But even then, please remember that the same sub should not visit your chapter more than once a month.

So next time you need a substitute – make them a great addition to the meeting!

Show me the money!

11/2/08

There are many reasons for joining BNI, but top of the list has to be more business. That's how you really know when things are working, when that cheque hits your bank account.

It surprises me that so many members seem reluctant to use the 'Show me the Money' box. Maybe it's the name. I think 'Thank You For The Business' would be better, or maybe it's just that people don't really know what it is for.

A member said to me last week that when the box first came round he thought it was some kind of collection box and you had to put money in it – like an extra collection at church. Again this has to be down to bad explanation or understanding. Either way it's a loss for the chapter. The box really needs to be used to the maximum, as it's not only like a testimonial to BNI, but more importantly proof of how well your Chapter is working for everyone. Not only is it a visible way of saying 'thank you' for referrals, but it also puts a value on the business being done in your group.

Imagine if the Membership Co-ordinator opens the box at the end of the month and announces that there are thank yous in the box totalling over £50k. What will that say to you? And if there are visitors in the room? Well, if it were me, I'd want to join on the spot!

So next time that box is passed to you at breakfast, don't reach for a £1 in your pocket. Take a card and thank a member for that referral they gave you that changed into real business.

That Referral yellow copy

14/2/08

Have you ever wondered why you get to keep the yellow copy of the Referral set?

I expect that at your Member Success training you were told that it was so that you could keep track of your referrals and, like a great deal of the information you were given that evening, the importance of it was lost on you.

Well, if like a great many members you just tuck it away somewhere and never look at it again, I want you from today to consider its real value.

If you ask the Membership Co-ordinator, they can tell you (from the PALMS report) how many referrals you have given in, say, the last month, last six months, in fact ever since you became a member. But, at least without a great deal of effort, that's about it.

However, if you make a record of those yellow slips you can see who you are giving referrals to and who you aren't. You can see how many referrals you are giving to each member and how often.

But the most crucial thing you can do in my mind is to use the yellow copy to follow up on every referral you give! And the best way that I have found to do this is by sending a quick email to the person I gave the referral to (two or three days later) saying something like '.. I was just wondering how you got on with my referral...' Then, if for some reason, your referral has been overlooked the person is straight on the phone and putting it right.

The result: your contact gets a better service, the person you gave the referral to increases their chance of winning the business and you get to give more referrals.

I'll explain that last comment next time.

Lost for ever!

15/2/08

You get a referral and for some reason you don't follow up on it.

It may be that you are just too busy, it's not really your type of work, it's only a small job and you don't really want it, you lose the details, any one of a hundred reasons. But whatever you do, whatever it takes, you must follow up on every referral that you are given!

If you are too busy, let the person know. If it's not really your type of work or too small a job, let them know – maybe you could even recommend someone else. If you lose the details call the Membership Co-ordinator and ask for them. Call the MC rather than the member who gave you the referral, as by calling the member and telling them that you lost the referral they gave (that they may have worked hard for), you are showing them that you didn't really value their referral.

But why should we do this? Well, there are two really important reasons – one impacts on the Giver and the other on the Receiver.

The way it affects the Receiver is easy. If that person gains a reputation as a person who doesn't follow up on referrals, what do you think will happen? The referrals stop coming!

But how it affects the Giver is almost undetectable but can have an unbelievable effect on the whole chapter – not just one person. And this I learnt the hard way!

I gave a referral to my next door neighbour and didn't follow it up. Three weeks later I bumped into them and asked how they had got on, only to find out that they had not even been contacted. Embarrassed, I got on to the member concerned and asked what had happened – they had been too busy. Anyway, they promised to call immediately. I checked with my neighbour the next day and sure enough the member concerned had rung, apologised and made an appointment.

But they failed to turn up!

A few months later my neighbour was having some more work done and I recommended someone else from my chapter, their reply '...what like that last one?!' Since then my neighbour has had the following jobs done: new bathroom, garden cleared, house decorated, plans for an extension drawn, building work, loan and who knows what else. All lost because a referral was not followed up and now my recommendations cannot be trusted!

So please, whatever it takes, follow up on every single referral that you are ever given.

Miss three meetings and you are out!

17/2/08

I've heard this often when talking to people about why they wouldn't join BNI (in fact even members worry about it) and again I can't understand where these ideas come from.

In all the time that I have been in BNI I don't remember anyone being asked to leave our chapter for being absent three times. More than three yes, but certainly not just three.

The whole belief structure of BNI is about helping its members to get the most from their membership and if, for some reason, members don't achieve this, then it is up to the Leadership Team, the Membership Committee and the chapter's Regional Director to help.

When a member is absent, the first thing that happens is that someone from the chapter will call to see if all is ok. If the member is absent again, they will again be called but also receive a letter reminding them of the

BNI policy regarding being absent. If absent again, obviously a stronger letter is sent.

So my question is: what is wrong with that? If a member is offered help every time they are absent and then they are again absent, what is that member saying about the offer of help? I would suggest that they don't care.

But the more important thing is this: I can tell you that a good member never gets to the stage of being asked to leave. Why? Well, first they will always find a substitute and yes, I know emergencies happen, but honestly how many on the actual day of your chapter meeting in a six-month period? And you can always get a substitute if you really want to – we had a member once who had to suddenly fly home to Japan. Do you think he didn't have a substitute for the next meeting? Of course not. He arranged one by email. We have another great member who unexpectedly had a site meeting the following morning (his BNI day), which he found out about at six in the evening. He made a quick phone call and his fellow members found him a substitute.

And just recently, a member had a major problem at home during the night, but they still had the thought to send a quick text saying sorry that they would miss the meeting. What do you think happened? Because they were a brilliant member and we had a number of visitors at our meeting that morning we asked one of them to substitute for them.

So, you see if you are a good member you would never get to your third absence! And even if you did, the Chapter's Leadership Team and Membership Committee would know that it really must have been out of your control and would, therefore, take that into consideration.

I've been in BNI for five years now and the absence rule has never worried me, nor do I think it should worry you.

For your information here is our actual rule.

Rule 5
Attendance is critical to the group. If a member cannot attend, they may send a substitute (not a member of their own Chapter) to the meeting. This will not count as an absence. A member is allowed three absences in any six month period. More than this and the member is subject to removal by the Chapter's Leadership Team or Membership Committee.

Givers Gain!

21/2/08

We have a great photographer in one of my chapters, but not only is he good behind his lens he is also wonderful in the chapter.

He rarely misses a meeting, is always one of the first members to arrive in the morning and always offers to help out.

When he had been a member a few weeks I suggested that he bring his camera and take a few pictures for our web site. The following week he arrived with his camera. A while later I cheekily asked if I could borrow one of his cameras (I do have a City and Guilds in Photography) to take some freebie shots for someone and he offered to take them for me – free of charge.

When I was looking for a photographer to take the photos at a charity 5k run I was organising, he offered to help without any hesitation, whereas another photographer (now an ex-member) turned down the opportunity.

More recently, he made a video for the chapter which he has since put on YouTube and then just last week he did one of the best 10 Minutes I have ever seen. He set up a studio, took some photos as he explained how he ran a function and ended up by giving every member a framed print of the group (a picture he had taken a few moments earlier).

Last week I was able to give my first real photography referral. There was only ever going to be one person I would give it to since he has given so much to me and the chapter and I have to say it felt really good to be able to give a referral that I had made a special effort to find.

Trouble getting to training?

24/2/08

Statistics show that successful chapters have higher attendance at the BNI workshops, yet it can still be difficult to motivate some members to attend.

The reasons seem to be many and varied, ranging from *"I'm too busy"*, *"I've been before"* (two years ago), *"I get better training at work"*, to *"Why would I want to learn BNI stuff?"* and just plain apathy.

Frankly, most of the reasons are just excuses, since if you really want to do something you make the time. *"I've been before"* – well, in my book that doesn't stand up either, as taken to its logical conclusion why would you ever do anything more than once? I've been to most of the BNI workshops at least once (Member Success three or four times) and each time I go there is something new I pick up. Sometimes it's just a sentence that makes it worth while and of course each time I go there are new members to network with.

"I get better training at work" – when I heard that one, I nearly .... well let's just say I wasn't amused! I could write for the next hour what I think about that remark but all I will say is that I would be surprised. I don't care what company you work for, BNI have some of the best trainers around and I will accept that you don't get Dr. Ivan Misner every work-shop or for that matter Andy Bounds, author of the best selling book the Jelly Effect, but you do get part of an excellent team. And even if you do believe that your training is better, how about going along because you are part of a team?

And, *"Why would I want to learn that BNI stuff, it's just for BNI, right?"* No, no it isn't! Presentation Skills, one of the BNI workshops, not worth it?! Are you really trying to tell me you only present yourself at BNI? What about at your next business meeting, when you are asked to give a speech at your best mate's wedding, or like me when for the first time I stood up in front of forty actors and told them how I was going to produce their show. Presentation skills are for every aspect of your life, not just at BNI. The same is true of the other workshops. So please attend them all. Not only will your chapter benefit, but so will you.

Apathy – this is a hard one to fight and many suggestions have been made to overcome it. Some chapters just announce the workshops, others send round a list for members to tick the ones they want to attend, some groups give each member a training schedule and ask them to mark off workshops and hand it back. I know of a chapter that tried booking every member on to a workshop and then told them to cancel if they couldn't go – I'm not sure myself that that's a great idea, as for BNI to get a block booking and then have people slowly cancel must be a real pain.

However, an idea that I heard about this week and one that is working to good effect, is where the Membership Co-ordinator just rings each member up and asks them if they want to attend the next workshop – yes or no – and then books them in. It's that simple and is having incredible results.

So if your chapter could benefit from some more training, why not try just picking up the phone?

When a few words say it all!

26/2/08

About a year ago a member in my chapter got up to do his 60 Seconds, placed his hands on the table in front of him and just looked about. After a few seconds the rest of the members started to look at each other and shrug, after another ten seconds there were a few nervous laughs and yet the member still stood there, from time to time turning their head from side to side. It was almost half way through the minute before the member spoke and then all he said was, *"Can't hear a thing, can you? Just listen"*. Now we all listened and sure enough you couldn't hear a thing and then the member spoke again, this time saying, *"That's because this room is double-glazed. So if you know someone that is fed up with hearing all the noise outside their home then get them to contact ..."*

Recently, another member bet me that she would get a standing ovation at our next meeting. In the five years that I have been a member no one else had, so I didn't see how a new member was going to achieve this at her second meeting. At the next meeting she asked everyone to stand, she then moved to the front of the group and said that she was going to show us a simple warm-up routine. This involved us putting our hands above our heads and slowly moving our arms backward and forward. This we did for a few moments and then she said, *".. a bit faster, that's it, now a bit faster ..."* and guess what? She got her standing ovation!

And then last week I called on a member to do their 60 Seconds. He nodded back to me and just sat there reading his paper. After a while he glanced at his watch but carried on reading. This group had all heard the double-glazing story so we all sat and waited, but thirty seconds passed and this member just carried on reading, in complete silence. At forty-five seconds we just didn't know what to expect. Then at fifty seconds he glanced at his watch again, folded his paper, looked up and said, *"Don't waste your time, speak to RBS instead!"* That was it, but he received rapturous applause. And what amazing nerve that took.

The one thing that these 60 Seconds have in common is that they will be remembered. Hardly a week goes by without me telling someone the double-glazing story. And on one of those occasions it resulted in £4,500 worth of work for the member and, because I keep talking about these 60 Seconds, they keep on working for the members concerned.

So next time you do your 60 Seconds dare to be different and do something that your fellow members will still be talking about in years to come.

Hate the thought of doing your 10 Minutes?

2/3/08

Many new members, and for that matter, some long standing members, hate the idea of having to do their 10 Minutes. In fact, some positively avoid it. And, having been one of those, I have to say I completely understand the feeling.

But time has changed that. Partly by attending the workshops, (although these really improve your presentation, rather than actually getting you to do a 10 Minutes in the first place), partly by watching other members do theirs, partly by the improvements made when doing my 60 Seconds and becoming more comfortable, but mainly by discovering a plan and having a great idea.

The plan is all about preparation and keeping things simple, about not making things complicated and trying to cram everything you know into 10 Minutes. Ensure the timing is right and practise until you feel happy with the way it sounds. Run your 10 Minutes in private: it's surprising how different things are when said out loud rather than just read. Practise your presentation in front of a friend if you can and ask for feedback – I hadn't realised that I danced backward and forward constantly and touched my nose a lot until a very good friend told me.

However, the thing that I have suggested to most people who have hated the idea of ten minutes when they are the centre of attention, is to have a great idea. Something that will make them forget their nerves and make them feel totally at home.

One great example of this was a decorator. Now let's be honest, not many decorators get up in front of a room full of people and tell them about their business – but that's what we do in BNI. So I suggested that they wallpaper a wall! Well not a wall exactly, but a sheet of board. When it came to the day, they were tense; the first minute of their presentation was nervy, but once they picked up their paste brush they were in their element! It was a brilliant 10 Minutes and everyone saw at first hand how good they were at their job.

So, as they say, think outside of the box, for a great and fun 10 Minutes.

The Winning Team

3/3/08

For the past two years BNI teams have taken part in the NBFA 5k Charity Fun Run held in Bushy Park (Teddington), near Hampton Court, South West London, during June.

The NBFA (National Benevolent Fund for the Aged) was founded to improve the quality of life for older people in the UK who live on a low income. This they do by providing direct, practical assistance through the provision of emergency alarms, TENS pain relief machines and the organisation of free holidays.

By taking part, BNI teams not only help to raise thousands of pounds for this wonderful charity, but also have lots of fun and some very competitive racing! Any number of runners (or walkers) can be in a team – so a whole chapter can take part – with only the first four home, from each team, scoring points. The BNI team with the best (lowest) score wins the trophy!

Last year's winning team was Business Class from Twickenham, Middlesex (see the photograph on the following page).

The best thing about this event is that everyone can take part: both young and not so young. The youngest runner last year was just eight and the eldest sixty-two, and also the fast and those just a little slower! The fastest runner last year finished in just over eighteen minutes and those that walked the route took just under fifty minutes.

And the best part? After the race you can picnic in the beautiful park with the family, take a walk along the river and watch the swans, visit Hampton Court Palace or just flop into one of the local pubs!

If you would like to enter a team in this year's event and try to beat the team from Business Class – on Sunday 8th June – just ask your Regional Director to get you some entry forms or contact BNI Head Office.

No 10 Minutes!

4/3/08

I can never really understand why this ever happens, or at least why anyone other than the Leadership Team knows the 10 Minutes speaker is missing for some reason.

The first thing the Leadership Team should know is who is the 10 Minutes speaker at that day's meeting and as soon as that member arrives check that all is okay. If for some reason the member doesn't show, then the

Chapter Director should always have a 'Chapter 10 Minutes' ready and announce it as if that was how it was always going to be. Not 'Oh. Fred hasn't turned up this morning, don't know where he is, so I'll fill in with something ..' What does that look like?

What is a 'Chapter 10 Minutes'? Well, it could be a short Power 1-2-1 session, or a session on Power Groups, or a session on the four workshops. Just something prepared and sitting in the chapter box waiting for the day that an emergency happens.

But what happens more often with a 10 Minutes is no Bio or Door-Prize or in fact both and this is so easy to avoid.

What I found worked well, when I was Treasurer, was this. The day after the meeting I would email the next speaker reminding them that it was their 10 Minutes the following week, enclosing a Bio sheet, asking for its return and reminding them to bring a wrapped door-prize.

Then the day before the meeting I would send them another email. This time asking if all was okay for the meeting the next day, saying thank you for their Bio (or not as the case may be) and finishing with something like, 'Looking forward to seeing what your door-prize is.'

By doing it this way, any problems came to light then, not the next morning, so a stand-in speaker could be found if needed, a Bio quickly written and a forgotten door-prize found.

How much better than no speaker, a forgotten Bio, or no door-prize. We have a Sightpath Business Catalyst in one of my chapters and his memory hook is 'Success comes to those who plan for it' and in this case the planning is so simple!

Hi,

I love your blog - very inspirational. We launched our own blog site here in NZ last week and I am still very much finding my way. I would welcome any feed-back if you get a moment.

All the best,
Graham Southwell
BNI New Zealand
www.bniblog.co.nz

I only buy from ….!

I was at a training recently given by Phil Berg, a great AD (Area Director) and also a brilliant educator, and there was a general all things BNI Q and A session going on.

Amongst other things that came up was how Phil found visitors. Being a Gold Badge holder (you receive a gold badge once you have invited six members into your Chapter), this is something that Phil is particularly good at, and the following idea of his is just so simple and has led to visitors for him.

We have all had the phone call when someone is trying to sell us something. Phil doesn't waste time trying to get rid of them, or eventually just hanging up on them, he just states instead that he only buys from BNI members and then asks if they are a BNI member.

What a great idea! And if they ask what BNI is, he says, *"Why not come along and find out?"*

Why not give it a try? You never know, it may help you on your way to a Gold Badge!

Don't be so polite!

10/3/08

Let's be realistic, referrals can at times be hard to find and other than those referrals that you get from someone who asks you if you know a good whatever it may be, you have to work for them. Obviously once you are tuned into the idea of referrals it's not hard work, but you still need to be actively switched into referral mode.

For most of us, this is something that has to be learned, and I can't recommend highly enough the Referral Skill workshop. In fact I would almost go as far as saying that this workshop should be made compulsory, as a member's ability to pass referrals directly affects the success of my membership, whereas their networking and presentation skills, on the other hand, only affects their likeihood of receiving referrals.

However, back to finding referrals. At the workshop you will be shown many ways of finding referrals, including some that require no work at all. Some of these ideas are what BNI like to call silent referral generation, and I have one that you may like to try.

All members are given a BNI business card wallet where they keep the cards of all the people in their chapter, so that when needed they have a member's card with them. Well, the first thing that I would suggest is that you have two or three of these wallets (you can buy them from your RD for a few pounds), and pass them around.

But this is my silent referral generator. Always have your BNI wallet on the passenger seat of your car (van) and the next time you give someone a lift, don't be polite and pick it up and throw it on the back seat. Let your passenger pick it up. They will then wonder what they should do with it and that's your opening!

You say, *"Oh, sorry, that's my BNI folder. It's full of the business cards of people I know and trust and are great at their jobs. Would you like to have a look?...."*

Why no rewards?

12/3/08

This question has come up a few times recently and is very easy to answer – BNI is based on recommending people you know, like and trust, not those that give you a 'thank you'.

Obviously no-one is going to worry about a bottle of wine, or similar, but when these 'thank yous' get bigger and expected, even arranged, well, that's when the problems start.

I'm not even going to go down the tax/legal route as that is outside my area of knowledge, although I would guess it's not good, but on the BNI front, what would it say if we recommended someone from whom we were getting a 'present'? Could our judgement be trusted?

The person or company you recommended might be the best there is, but think about it from your own point of view. If you knew the person or company being recommended to you was being given a nice 'thank you' to do so, would you trust them?

I would suggest not!

Leadership Team Training

16/3/08

This week saw the new teams for April being trained and as always there are those members who when they agree to be on the new team then don't understand the need to attend training. The reason for not needing to is always the same: because they have been to the training before.

Even if you were to discount the fact that the training is always improving, that new procedures are announced, that members share their ideas and worries and these are discussed, that everyone in the new team has heard the same information at the same time and so are all working from a common knowledge base, what about the fact that this is TEAM training?

Everyone is part of the team and there is more to the training than just training. It's about team building and, exactly as in your chapter, you need to take part and show your commitment to the team. So the fact that you may have been to the training before may mean that you have some idea of what your job is all about, although I can guarantee you that you won't know it all, but more importantly missing the training gives out the wrong signal to the new team. Because I think what it says is that you are not really fully part of the team. You will do your job, but not a great deal more.

BNI is all about building relationships and you can't build relationships if you don't take part and work on them. For a Leadership Team to work really well every one of the members must work on building that team.

To all those that have trained this week, work hard on your team and your chapter will reap the rewards.

Don't forget to have some fun. Your six months will be up before you know it!

Write your own Bio

24/3/08

You have your 10 Minutes coming up and the Treasurer asks you to fill out a biography sheet, so you fill out the obligatory spaces on the form: spouse, children, animals, hobbies, other interests, burning desire, something no-one knows about you and your key to success. Then, if you are lucky and the treasurer can read your handwriting, it gets read out with some enthusiasm, something like this:

Spouse: Mary. Children, none. Animals, none. Hobbies, golf and football. Other Interests, most sport. Burning Desire, to travel. Something no-one knows about me, I once played for the Arsenal Youth team. Key to Success, always doing my best.

It's fine, but what is that adding to your presentation and, let's be honest, how often have you given the Treasurer the same biography sheet? In my Chapter members do that and what's more they don't even update their dates – so they have still been married three years when I know it's now four!

A 10 Minutes is just that, eight minutes and questions or a straight ten minutes. But a well written biography can add to that another minute or more, so make the most of it! Next time you have a 10 Minutes coming up and your Treasurer asks for a Bio, write it and make use of every word. The Treasurer can say things about you that you can't say yourself, so give them some good stuff and build up your image.

This is what I did for my last 10 Minutes:

David is married and has four boys, two of whom were born on the 23rd March – however they are not twins, the eldest being four years older than his brother!

He went to Hampton Infant and Junior schools, and then to Teddington senior school – via a two-year stopover at Rectory (now Hampton Community school). He also has a City & Guilds in photography and yachting exams up to Coast Skipper.

David loves to cook (especially fish) and enjoys cooking the recipes of Elizabeth David, Keith Floyd, Rick Stein and Delia Smith.

He is again this year organising the NBFA 5k charity run.

His key to success is never accepting second best!

Does he have a burning desire? Yes – but it will always remain a secret! David loves to write and currently has two blogs: My BNI Day and Convert to Imperial. And something that very few people know about him, is that he once wrote a children's story, which was printed monthly in the Horse Rangers' magazine, using a girl's name as a pseudonym. He would one day love to have the story published.

Follow your money!

30/3/08

Where to find visitors is a constant question I hear amongst members. Now I'm not going to tell you that finding visitors is easy, but neither do I believe that finding visitors is as hard as a lot of members think.

However, I do believe that a great many members chase the same potential visitors without success, so how about this for an idea? Follow your money.

So what do I mean by that? Well, where do you get and, more importantly, where do you spend your money? Take the last six months for example: where have you been spending your money? – business and personal. Have a look through your purchase ledger, invoices or your cheque book at home and see who you have paid and for what.

These people are your own personal visitor list, no one else has this exact list. And the best thing about this list is that you know all the people on it and how good they are at their job. You already have a relationship with them and so calling them is easy and, what's more, they will be happy to talk to you.

Tell them how happy you were with their work; ask them if they are looking for more business and ask them to your chapter.

So if you are stuck for ideas of where to find your next visitor, give this a try and I promise that you will be surprised at the results!

Thank you for the business!

3/4/08

The 'Show Me the Money' box (I think only used in UK Chapters) is a great idea but, as I have said before, it's surprising how many members don't really understand its use or value. Maybe if the box had been called 'Thank you for the business' which I like to call it, its use would have caught on faster and with less misinterpretation. But, as I say, if used correctly it's a great idea.

Using the box could not be more simple – as all you are doing is thanking a fellow member for a referral that has turned into real business, although even this seems open to debate as some members seem to find it hard to decide whose name to put on the card and exactly what amount. Both are easy; the name is the person you received the referral from and the amount is the figure on your invoice – before any VAT. So, if you are a florist it might be £50 for a bouquet of flowers, whereas for a builder it might be £60,000 for an extension. The amount is nothing to do with profit, it's simply the amount that you invoice or receive for your services – an IFA for example might be involved in a large deal, hundreds of thousands of pounds, but it is the fee that is earned that goes on the card.

As to the value of using the box – well, this can be really amazing if every member of a chapter uses the box to its full. Every week we pass referrals and hopefully lots of them. But at the end of the day, a Referral Slip is nothing more than a slip of paper, an opportunity to do business. But a card in the 'Show Me the Money' box is proof of actual business done!

Just imagine the impact on the members of a chapter, let alone the visitors, when a Membership Co-ordinator stands up and says, *"This month as a group we did £20,000 of business between us"*. And, what if the MC said it was £30,000 or even £50,000? So, next time the box is passed to you at a meeting please use it, don't just pass it on!

All locked up!

9/4/08

When I arrived at my BNI meeting last week, I was late as it was 6.40am. I was therefore surprised to find the car park full of members! For some reason our venue was closed and we were left standing in the cold – visitors as well.

At ten to seven the doors were still locked and it was time for some quick thinking! So our Chapter Director rang a local pub he knew and asked the landlord if he fancied getting out of bed and opening up to give twenty plus people breakfast. He said yes!

So with a lot of car sharing we drove the few minutes to our substitute venue, where the landlord produced some wonderful coffee and Danish pastries for all. We had a great meeting, a good number of referrals, and our visitors enjoyed it – one submitted an application after the meeting and another is coming back with his next week.

Not something I would want to do every week, but as a team-building event it was pretty good!

World record?

14/4/08

At our meeting two weeks ago a member – Gareth Miller (Garden Designer) – gave 85 referrals. Yes, I did say eighty five!

It was truly amazing. I've seen over twenty referrals given before, but eighty five? Well, that is just outstanding and, what's more, the average number for our whole chapter for a month.

Now I know what people are thinking – were they really referrals? All I can say is that my company, Imperial Printers, was lucky enough to receive twenty of the referrals (in response to my 10 Minutes presentation two weeks before) and every single person I called was not only expecting my call, but, so far I have completed quotes for ten of the companies and also secured two jobs. So yes, I would say that they were all real referrals.

I guess you are thinking – so how did he do it?

Well, it seems that it was pretty simple! He just asked every single person he met or spoke to how he could help them: even his optician while he was having some new glasses fitted. And once he got going, he just couldn't stop!

Now I have to say that Gareth is a natural and, for many of us asking such a question of everyone we met would be way out of our comfort zone. But how about trying to ask just one person a day how you could help them?

You never know, you might just set a personal record!

Andy Bounds let me down!

16/4/08

I'm just back from the 11th Annual BNI Directors European Conference held this year in Dublin, where Andy Bounds (communications expert and writer of a best selling book) was one of the main speakers.

Now I'm not going to try and tell you he was a bad speaker, because he was brilliant! His understanding of what clients really want (he calls this the 'Afters'), and his ability to explain it in simple terms, is outstanding. He is not only entertaining but also very clear with his message.

And to be honest, if I don't both improve my BNI business and my printing business having heard him speak I ought to be shot!

However, it was the 'Afters' that got me. He explains that you don't buy a newspaper, you buy news. You don't buy glasses, you buy sight. And likewise, you don't buy a communications expert (Andy Bounds), you buy the ability to communicate with your target audience. He further explains that you shouldn't provide what you think your customers want, it has to be what your customers perceive they want. You have to provide the correct 'Afters' to make them happy to buy from you.

This is where it all went wrong for me. At the end of his speech he asked for referrals into three banks and then left the stage to a standing ovation.

On my way out of the hall I spotted him at the rear of the hall signing books for a few people. I went up to him, waited my turn and when it came said how much I had enjoyed his presentation (as I had done to other speakers) and asked for his business card. He replied that he didn't have any, made a joke about it and then blanked me!

No 'If you have a pen take my email address' – just a big fat nothing. He then turned and proceeded to sign his book for another member. Now, for all he knows, I could have had a name at one of the banks he wanted to speak to, or I may have wanted to book him for a speaking engagement. I certainly didn't get the 'Afters' that I was hoping for and just ended up feeling that the last two hours had all been just a show, nothing more.

I feel rather sad about that.

Clapping adds energy!

20/4/08

I don't know what it is like in your region, but in mine the opinion as to whether members should clap after each 60 Seconds presentation is divided. The recommendation is that there be no clapping, but it is left to the individual chapters to decide for themselves. In mine we clap.

Now, there are various arguments for and against. On the against side the arguments seem to centre on timekeeping and the fact that even bad 60 Seconds get clapped, so how do you tell a good one?

But I think the reasons for clapping far outweigh those against. Firstly, I would suggest that if a Chapter is running over time due to clapping, then there is in fact a much larger problem somewhere else. As for the bad 60 Seconds getting clapped, well, I can assure you that it is easy to spot the difference between a bad 60 Seconds and a very good one.

But there is much more!

For one thing, just think about that new member, worried about their 60 Seconds presentation. How confidence building is it to get clapped for that first 60 Seconds? Then, to my mind, when I visit chapters that don't clap, the change over between speakers is just totally dead. You just get the noise of chairs being pushed back, paper rustling and members talking because they have nothing else to do. Clapping at its worst covers all of that and, what's more, uses the time to better effect. At its best, clapping builds on the energy already in the meeting and can even inject energy when it has been missing. And, another interesting thing I have noticed is that the 10 Minutes speaker is often better when there is real energy in the meeting.

So yes – I think clapping adds real energy to a meeting and I thank our RD for promoting it.

Too busy for a One2One!

22/4/08

A member asked me recently what they should do, as a couple of members in their chapter had told them that they were too busy for a One2One and another said that they didn't do them.

My simple answer was to do nothing, just to move on and find someone who did want to do a One2One. But then I thought about it some more. What exactly are you saying if you don't have time for a One2One?

That you are not interested in finding your fellow member more referrals? That you yourself don't want that same member to find you more referrals?

But there is even more to it than that.

Obviously not having the time for a One2One is not going to increase the number of referrals you receive. But the more interesting question is, will it reduce the number of referrals that you receive? And I would suggest that it would!

Why? Well, on the most basic level, if you are too busy for a One2One then similarly you must be too busy to take on more work. Then, on a personal level, if you are too busy to spend some time with a member you are not exactly building goodwill and trust, a BNI ethic. But, more importantly, if the member feels snubbed – do you really think they are going to try and find you referrals? So whenever you are asked for a One2One, even if you really are too busy, take the time to make a date in your diary. Six weeks time is far better than never! And I also think that you will be pleased with the result.

No badge equals less money!

17/05/08

Some of our members see no value in wearing a badge: they think it's one of 'those' BNI rules. I know of at least one member who refuses to wear a badge, because he is above that kind of thing. He's his own man! Well, all I can say is that he, and those like him, are ...... well let's just say, they don't get 'it' at all!

So the question is, why do we wear a badge? Is it that BNI like their little rules? Their little symbols of corporate being? Is just to make us feel stupid? Well, the answer is no, no and no.

Now I expect that both Martin Lawson and Ivan Misner could write a book on the benefits of wearing a badge. However, I would just like you to think about these few things and then tell me you don't think our BNI badges are a good idea.

A major part of our weekly meetings is for the benefit of visitors and after that our new members; they have never seen BNI or us before. So what better way of making people feel at ease than a badge with your name clearly printed on it? And from your own point of view, isn't it easier if a new member has their name on a badge in case you can't remember it? From my own point of view, as a Regional Director I have to confess that sometimes I can't remember the name of every single member in all of my Chapters, so it really helps me if a member wears their badge.

But if you want the most compelling reason of all as to why you should wear a badge - it's because if you don't, it will cost you money!

How? How could such a little thing cost you money?

Well, all the things above have have one thing in common. And, I have done it on many occasions myself and I know many other people that have also. I've walked into a room full of people, walked towards two people - both whom I knew - but I couldn't remember their names. One wasn't wearing a badge, the other was and I could see their name clearly. Which do I talk to? And, more importantly, which one gets to tell me about their business and what they are looking for? To grow a relationship with me?

I think we all know the answer! I may have been just the person the person not wearing the badge needed to speak to that day, but we will never know. Possible business gone. Just for the sake of a badge!

So, do you think that BNI want us to wear a badge just to be difficult or because it just might increase our business gained from BNI? I'll leave you to decide!

One of your fellow members is holding an event

1/06/08

I happened to be talking with four members this week who had all had the same experience. I met with them on different days by the way!

They had each held an event, were in chapters of over twenty members, and each event was free. Two of these events were evening sessions, one spread over three days and the other one was in fact online. The number of members from their Chapters who chose to support them ranged from none (on two occasions) to about five!

Amazed? Well, I was!

Why? Well, let's start with building a supportive relationship. How about it's just a friendly thing to do, or how about the fact that you might just learn something (two of the events were about growing your business), or a bit selfish - for the networking possibilities. Then again how about the fact that there can be no better way to learn about a person's business than watching them work – what a great way to get an insight into how they work, understanding what they do, and so increase the chance of getting referrals for them. Or how about just because you may get to know them a little more?

Something that is very important in our groups, which also impacts directly on how many referrals we receive, is how much we know, like and trust our fellow members.

How do you think those four members feel? Deep down - do you really think they like us? Do you really think that they will go out of their way to find us referrals?

Next time one of your fellow members is holding an event, posts something on the web for you to look at, or even asks you just to have a look at their web site, please really try to find the time to do whatever it is. I guarantee that, at the very least, you will make a member happy and by doing that, you will certainly increase the odds of a referral or two from them.

Super Sub!

8/6/08

I was at a chapter recently who had a 'Super Sub' and I really mean a Sub who was super. (More about the other kind another time.)

This guy was really amazing. The story started some weeks before when he was asked to be a subsitute for a member but forgot to turn up. Obviously the member was marked as absent. Well, the member when he found out wasn't too impressed and let his subsitute know!

So next time the member wanted a Sub, whom did he call? Yes, the same person.

And, this was the meeting that I was attending. When the subsitute was called to read out the member's 60 Seconds, it was great, but about half way through the 60 Seconds it then told us that this was the person who had let the member down and we could be as horrible to him as he deserved! He finished and sat down; brave to read it if you ask me.

After the members, as there was no clash, the subsitute was asked to give his 60 Seconds. He introduced himself, told us what he did and then picked up two bags and started to give out bottles of wine. Everyone received a bottle and it was his way of saying sorry to the member and us for letting the Chapter down!

Amazing and what a way to be remembered! And I've kept his card, because if he cares that much, I bet he also cares about his job!

Team spirit!

16/06/08

Five BNI teams, plus three members of staff from BNI Head Office, took part in the NBFA Charity 5k on Sunday 8th June. The weather was perfect and the competitive spirit increased, as the 10 o'clock start time got nearer.

Along with Charlie Lawson, Tim Cook (both Assistant National Directors) and Kathleen Waller from Head Office, were teams from Tudor (including LNW Area Director Dinah Liversidge), Business Class, Platinum, Swan and Iolanthe (who had only just launched on the 5th June).

For Tudor and Business Class this race (to date anyway) was a decider, as Tudor had won the first NBFA race in 2006 and Business Class took the winner's trophy in 2007. Both chapters had entered a good number of runners and on paper Tudor were the stronger team. However, even before the starter had said 'Go', Tudor had lost two of their runners: one to a twisted knee, the other to Glyndebourne.

John Wilson (Tudor) led, by bicycle, the first runners round the beautiful tree lined course in Bushy Park in what was to be a very fast time for the winner: Daniel Bent a teacher from a local school – his time 17m 28sec.

Chris Lovelock (CJL Construction) of the Tudor Chapter came home in 6th place in a brilliant sub twenty-minute time (19m 54sec) and the stage was set for an easy Tudor victory. But then in 20th place and 22nd place came two Business Class runners and things were once again looking interesting. It now all rested on the finishing positions of the remainder of the four person teams. Things once again looked like a certain win for Tudor when they took the 35th position, but this was quickly followed by Business Class taking 38th. Then disaster struck. News came through that Mark Archer (Tudor) had pulled up with a torn calf-muscle – he had been looking at a good finish of around 30th. The Tudor team had been reduced to just four runners and now it was all down to those last few finishers.

The result was close, very close, but Business Class came from behind to snatch the trophy out of Tudor's hands!

There were other notable performances on the day: Tim Cook finished in 24th place in a time of 23m 47sec, just seeing off one of his members at the Swan Chapter. Charlie Lawson finished! I don't say this lightly as Charlie had been in Paris for a stag party on the Saturday evening, caught a plane home at 6.00 am Sunday morning and came directly to the race. He reckoned that most of the alcohol was out of his system by the time he had finished! It would also appear that Kathleen had been at a hen party until 4.00 am on the Sunday morning – so her finishing position of 53rd in a time of 26m 43sec was pretty outstanding.

Dinah walked the course – aided by personal trainer Katy Spragg (Business Class) – in just under an hour and finished to great applause. It was the furthest she had walked in over 14 years.

Tom Tree (Platinum) got more than a referral – after he had finished, his legs hurt rather a lot and so he took advantage of the free massage being given by some lovely ladies – he now has a date with one of them! And last was Veronica Lartey (Iolanthe). Having got lost on the way to the race she started half an hour late, but still wanted to take part. She crossed the line to a BNI guard of honour.

The 8th June was a great success for the NBFA as they raised lots of funds for our older folks, but it was also a great day for BNI, as all the members showed what having fun, teamwork and wonderful support is all about.

Thank you to everyone that took part and.... see you all again next year!

Photographs of the event, taken by John Frye (Tudor), can be seen at: http://www.johnfrye.co.uk/NBFA%205k/index.html

Annoyed by talkers?

18/6/08

Have you ever felt yourself getting hot under the collar because someone at the next table is always talking through the 60 Seconds presentations?

And, I'm not talking here about the odd whisper to a visitor to explain what's going on in the meeting, I'm talking about that member who talks at their normal volume as if nothing else in the room is going on.

It never fails to astound me that these people don't realise that they are making it almost impossible for those around them to concentrate on the content of the speakers' 60 Seconds being given. They have little chance of finding referrals for their fellow members because they have no idea what the members are actually looking for.

But, the thing that really gets me, is that they don't understand that the chances of me looking for a referral for someone that is so rude, is, well, about zero! So if you are one of the 'talkers' in your chapter and you often wonder why you don't get as many referrals as you think you should – well, you may now just have the answer!

Anyone for tennis?

22/6/08

A great 60 Seconds will keep bringing you referrals for years!

I was at a chapter this week and we were about half way through the 60 Seconds presentations when this guy stood up, pushed a head band over his wavy hair, picked up a tennis racket and cried *"You cannot be serious!"*

He then handed another racket to an accomplice, produced a tennis ball and together they played a rally (in fact several) down the centre of the tables.

He is a music teacher (piano, saxophone and clarinet) and band member who was promoting one of his gigs which was taking place the following week.

Why the tennis? Well, his gig is next week and the Wimbledon Lawn Tennis championships start next week. Being a tennis fan (he has tickets to semi-final day), and believing that you could not be serious if you were thinking of missing his band perform, well, John McEnroe just popped into his head!

It was the most memorable 60 Seconds of the day: I have already re-told it to a number of people and I am writing about it here.

Like all good stories that get told time and time again, I will talk about this 60 Seconds many times over the coming years and each time it will be a referral opportunity. So, get creative and keep those referrals coming in!

Joseph Marshall and his Band, Ramajaz, are playing at the George IV, Chiswick, on Wednesday 2nd July from 8.00pm.
Email: josephjmarshall@hotmail.com

What have you been doing for the last 10 years?

24/6/08

Of course, this question could even be five, ten, fifteen or twenty years, but the question remains. Do you ever ask your fellow members what they used to do?

I ask this because I heard recently of a member who was thinking of leaving BNI because there was no-one he had met who matched his needs – basically because they were all small businesses.

When questioned about this and asked to name someone he wanted to meet he replied that there was no point as 'you wouldn't know the kind of person I need to speak to'.

The lady member concerned (she runs a small roofing company) asked if he would humour her and give her a name of someone that would be a good contact for him. He said that he couldn't see the point, but if he must – Glaxo SmithKline would be a great contact.

I don't know the actual outcome of this story, but I do know that the lady concerned had been the World Events organiser for Glaxo SmithKline for over 10 years!

Do you think that she probably knew someone that the member would have loved to talk to?

So, never assume that a member is only what they are today. Ask the question, and you may just be very surprised!

Love this post!
Can I use it in SuccessNet?
Dr. Ivan Misner, Founder BNI

A picture paints a thousand words!

27/6/08

I was at a meeting recently when a member stood up to give his 60 Seconds. He is a photographer.

He read it, as many members do, from a prepared script, but the script wasn't scribbled on the back of a referral slip, on a creased piece of paper, or for that matter on a lovely crisp typed sheet of paper. It was on the back of a beautiful photograph.

The photograph faced us and everyone got to see it as he turned around the group in order to have addressed all of us.

Brilliant!

Not only was his 60 Seconds good, but what a demonstration of both his work and his preparation skills. No-one in his group could be left with any doubt as to whether they should recommend him.

Okay, we are not all so lucky as to be a photographer and have wonderful pictures to sell us. But, if you are going to use a script why not put it on the back of a nice card with your company logo on the front?

Presentation and branding is so important to every business, however small or large, so what a great and really simple way to raise your image within your Chapter.

Air conditioning not working

1/7/08

Recently I had a One2One with a member who owns a lawn-cutting franchise. After we had finished and as I was near to the garage where I have my car serviced and its air conditioning was playing up – it was acting more like a heater – I decided to see if they could have a look at it for me.

Having been a customer for many years they said that they could have a look at it on the spot. I watched the mechanic at his work for a few minutes, but could soon tell that all was not going well, so took myself off to wait in reception.

I got bored watching the receptionist type invoices and began to think about lawns – I really wanted to get this member a referral or two. But where to start?

After a while it struck me that I had a captive audience – the receptionist – there was no telling who she might know! So, I stood up, crossed over to her desk, and said, *"Excuse me. I don't suppose you know someone with a large garden and a lawn that needs cutting?"* She said, *"No"*, looking somewhat surprised, so I sat down again.

A couple of minutes passed before my failure began to play on my mind. I couldn't give up; after all there were lots of members I could find referrals for. So I crossed to the receptionist again, this time I said, *"Sorry to disturb you again, but as well as this brilliant lawn cutting company I work with a number of other really great local business owners, such as a plumber, tiler, electrician, bank, IFA, web designer…So if you need any of those…?"*

"No", she said again. Not to be totally defeated I suggested that now that she knew that I knew loads of good business people that she could call me if a need ever came up. She smiled and said *"Of course"*.

Just as I was about to return to my chair, she said, *"I need a couple of doors repaired in my hallway at home. Have you a carpenter that you would recommend?"*

We have a wonderful carpenter in my chapter, so I gave her his details, got her details for him which included the best time to call her at work. At that moment the mechanic appeared at the door to say that he had discovered the fault on my car and that they would have to order a part.

I left my garage a few minutes later feeling really pleased, as I had a referral to take to my chapter meeting the next morning and the best thing? It had cost me nothing to get it – just a little thought!

Referral possibilities are everywhere, and not always where you expect. It's just that sometimes you may have to get a little out of your comfort zone to find them!

Your actions in this scenario are EXACTLY what BNI is all about!!! Nice job.
Dr. Ivan Misner
Founder, BNI

Sharp intake of breath!

4/7/08

Have you ever been at a meeting where a visitor gets up to do their 60 Seconds and as soon as they mention what they do, there is a sharp intake of breath around the room?

The visitor clashes with one of the members of the chapter and that member is looking like thunder! I've witnessed this; I've even witnessed a similar reaction when a clash has been discovered at the sign-in table (this was followed with a great deal of rushing about the room by the member concerned telling everybody that would listen that the visitor couldn't speak).

But what I've never understood is why these members get so upset.

If it happened to me - I would of course have a quiet word with the member who had invited the visitor after the meeting and find out why they thought that there wasn't a clash. But that's about it.

Now you might be thinking that I'm mad – but think about it for a minute.

I've been a member of my Chapter for five years, I have good relationships with most of the members, some of the members are good friends of mine, and my company Imperial Printers I believe is well respected.

Is it really likely that if another printer got up and did a 60 Seconds that all the members of the chapter would suddenly flood that person with referrals?

I don't think I really need to answer that question – but if it ever happens to you, don't worry about it, be calm and polite. After all, however good they may turn out to be, they can't come back a second week!

Referral Reality Check

12/7/08

This week I was at a meeting when during the Referral Reality Check section the details of a referral from the previous week were read out and the recipient asked how things were progressing. Nothing wrong with that. However, what followed really demonstrated the benefit of the part of any BNI meeting.

The member that had received the referral said that as yet nothing had happened – he had not been contacted. At this the member who had given the referral got defensive about it and said that the member concerned had already been contacted. The member said no he hadn't! There then followed a couple of minutes of each member trying to prove their respective positions.

It turned out that the member who had received the referral had in fact been contacted! What caused the confusion was that he didn't know who was going to contact him and the person who did contact him (the member receives calls from a number of other sources) didn't know who had recommended him. In the end it was fine and the referral proved to be good.

But this situation could so easily have been avoided had the referral slip given been completed fully in the first place! So, next time, and every time, you give a referral please ensure that you give every piece of information needed to make the referral complete in itself.

And, one last idea that I have found useful: when giving a contact a member's business card – write your name on it.

How many times have you seen your favourite film?

20/7/08

I must have seen my favourite film at least a dozen times and I've watched every episode of The West Wing three times and each time I watch them

I notice something more. There are always bits I don't remember and, more often than not, parts that make more sense seen a second or third time in watching – the odd line that I didn't fully understand the significance of becomes clear.

The point is every time I watch I get more out of the film and in some ways it's more fun. Okay, I know who dies and how the film ends, who is going to be the next president in the West Wing, but let's face it, when 007 gets into a spot of bother we know he is going to be okay. We are just interested in how he will get out of it this time!

Now you may be thinking, that's all very well, but what has it got to do with BNI?

Well, it's amazing how many members I meet that say, *"Oh. I've done that workshop. Why would I want to go again?"*

Clearly there are the obvious reasons: workshops develop and change, the networking possibilities with a different set of members, motivation. But what about the simple fact that first time round you won't have taken everything in?

I've been to some workshops over half a dozen times and every time I pick up something new. Suddenly something will become crystal clear in my mind because the speaker explained it in a slightly different way. I'm reminded of something that I've stopped doing or in fact sometimes something I've never done.

You can only benefit from attending a workshop. So if not for your own business, please go along as often as you can for your fellow chapter members – you may just find that you benefit anyway!

I'm entitled!

26/7/08

This was something I was told was given as a reason for being absent from a meeting when the Membership Co-ordinator had rung a member to see if they were okay. The member was just taking one of the absences that they were entitled to. *Entitled!*

No! Sorry – a member is not entitled to any absences. The BNI Policy says – A member is allowed three absences in any six month period. And, the most important word there is 'allowed'.

But what I can't understand is why would you not want to go to your meeting in the first place?

Let's start with the selfish reason – the referrals that you might receive that week. Okay, so you might be thinking 'well they will contact me with any referrals I get given anyway' and I guess you would be right. But if you don't do a 60 Seconds that week – will anyone be able to find you referrals for next week?

What about the 10 Minutes presentation that you miss – do you think you will be top of the speakers list for referrals that week? – I don't think so.

And, what if the members find out that you didn't attend the meeting because you couldn't be bothered – do you think anyone will be looking out for referrals for you?

But, what about a more practical reason for not being 'just' absent?

Say you don't bother to attend your meeting one week – no reason, just don't feel like it. Then a couple of weeks later one of your children is sick and your really can't get to the meeting – a perfectly good reason. And, a couple of months later you go out to start the car and the battery is flat – another perfect reason for missing a meeting.

But, suddenly you have three absences against your name – your membership of the group is under threat. And, at the next committee meeting your attendance record is discussed – how will they view your commitment to the group.

Well, a committee member says *"the first absence was because they couldn't be bothered to turn up, fancied a morning off"*. If it were to come to the crunch – do you think that they would give you the benefit of the doubt?

I can tell you that the answer is – No!

So, no - you are not entitled to a single absence from your group, but you are allowed to be absent in an emergency.

To get the best from your group you have to build goodwill and trust – so please don't ever think that your are 'entitled' to miss a meeting.

David, love your blog message here. I'd like to link to it from one of our next newsletters. Is that OK with you?

Dr. Ivan Misner
Founder, BNI
July 26, 2008 3:14 PM

Topless!

27/7/08

Well, almost...

Katy Spragg our chapter's personal trainer (Fitness from the Heart) had a subsitute this week, a lady I knew from another local chapter.

Katy loves to get our pulses racing a little faster during her 60 Seconds, so often has the whole group up on our feet bending, stretching or jogging on the spot. However, even we had not expected what Clare Brown her Sub had in store for us.

When Clare was asked to give Katy's 60 Seconds she jumped on to her chair and asked everyone to stand. It was what happened next that will no doubt have this 60 Seconds talked about for months to come. She crossed her arms and whipped her t-shirt off over her head!

She then gave us a fifty second workout in just her bra and trousers that I can assure you not only got our heart rate up but also got a fair few members pretty warm!

Clare's 60 Seconds was followed by cheers and a great round of applause – we pitied the member that had to follow her with their 60 Seconds.

Not only will I remember Fitness from the Heart because of a great 60 Seconds but I will remember (for a very long time) Clare Brown from Morgan Brown - Reliable Female Decorators – 07966 166152.

So, be inventive and get remembered.

Over-saturation!

28/7/08

In my area (Twickenham, in South West London), every time visitors are mentioned, over-saturation of Chapters is also mentioned as a reason for not being able to get any.

Well, frankly that is rubbish!

Now, I'm not going to tell you that we should cram more and more Chapters into the area and I'm not going to give you the BNI statistic that says a population of so many thousand businesses will support this number of chapters. But, what I will tell you is this:

I have lived in this area for all of my life, through infant, junior, senior school and college. I have been a parent governor, commercial manager at Hampton FC, involved with the Horse Rangers, been the director for a local amateur dramatic group and played both cricket and basketball for local teams. And, more importantly, run my own business in the local area from the age of 21.

Added to this I have been a member of my BNI Chapter for over five years, as a BNI Regional Director help another three local Chapters, and have been to most of the other local chapters and workshops too many times to count. All of this leads me to my point – in all of that time, in meeting all of those people, I have only ever come across three people in BNI that I had known before!

And, another interesting fact – search on the web for builders in the TW area and you will find that there are over 350. Over-saturation? I don't think so.

Truth or Delusion?

16/08/08

One of the books I took on holiday with me recently was Dr. Ivan Misner's 'Truth or Delusion?' and I have to say that it is the best book I've read to date on networking and referral marketing.

If only I had read it the minute it was published, as without doubt I would be not only giving but gaining a great deal more from my BNI membership!

The book explains in clear and simple terms the not so obvious prerequisites for a good and effective networking system to work.

So, I really recommend that you get hold of this book without delay. You can't fail to benefit from reading it.

Birthday meeting

18/8/08

6th August was my birthday and the first meeting of the Faida Chapter in Nairobi (Kenya's second chapter).

A last minute business trip to Uganda gave me the chance to visit Kenya as well, and a quick check on the BNI web site, followed by an email to the National Director of Kenya (Muraguri E), resulted in the discovery that a BNI meeting was being held in the Sarova Panafric, the very hotel that I happened to be staying in. This was a coincidence too good to ignore.

And what a meeting it turned out to be!

Nineteen members, some excellent 60 Seconds, a very good Education Co-ordinator's slot by BNI Middle East National Director Bijay Shah on 'Luck' and a very clear 10 Minutes presentation, using PowerPoint, by Becky Nyamu on her company's signage products. The contribution part of the meeting provided nineteen referrals and some very worthwhile

'Show me the Money' slips. One of these was for 1.1 million Kenyan shillings (about £8000). Some of the visitors did think that this part of the meeting was time for another sales pitch, but Muraguri E (standing in as Chapter Director for this first meeting) soon sorted this out.

But all of this was nothing compared to the number of visitors in the room – forty! (They had had two hundred visitors at their launch the prevoius week). I've never seen so many application forms being filled in at a meeting before.

I left the meeting at 10.00am, having answered a great many questions on my five years in BNI. The room was still full and a committee meeting was in full swing – a pile of application forms in front of them.

From what I saw at this first meeting Douglas Wekhomba (CD), Vincent Lugalia (MC), Mike Kimundu (ST), the Leadership Team, and Muraguri E and the enthusiam of the members – BNI is set for big things in Kenya.

It's raining!

25/8/08

I'm sitting in my office gazing out of the window, looking at the rain bounce off the pavement. It was also raining last week when I visited the Iolanthe chapter in Hounslow (Middlesex, England), the members arriving as if they had taken a shower with their clothes on.

As I watched a lady run to her car it reminded me of an idea I had heard of at a training event that I had attended that week. It's a simple idea that the Visitor Hosts employ whenever there's the possibility of rain and what a great impression it must make on the visitors and members alike.

Two Visitor Hosts stand at the entrance with umbrellas and when someone arrives they go out to meet them and bring them back to the entrance of the venue and so into the meeting nice and dry! How good is that?

In fact this Chapter now has ten Visitor Hosts and each has a job – maybe something to think about for your group?

No visitors!

30/8/08

Can't think whom to invite to your next meeting? It's a problem that all of us have from time to time, believe me, even those lucky enough to wear a gold badge as I do.

But a great idea I heard recently when my Area Director, Dinah Liversidge, was asked this question at a recent training workshop may well help you.

What she advised was at the member's next chapter meeting, when the Secretary/Treasurer announces the next six 10 Minutes speakers, instead of listening for their name, she suggested that they write the six names down. Then the member would have a perfect list for people to invite to each meeting.

Who better to invite than someone in the speaker's power circle (not already in the chapter) or a potential customer for the speaker. If you have already been talking to someone about the speaker, what a great time to invite them along, to not only meet the member but also see their presentation.

I have to say that this is the best idea that I have heard in a long time. It benefits so many people - the visitor, the member who is speaking, obviously your chapter, and you the member. And, won't that member thank you if your visitor turns into business for them?!

No Door Prize!

5/9/08

I'm often asked what's the point of the Door Prize and I have to say that it's one of the few occasions on which I am almost lost for words! Why?

Well, for a start three reasons I suppose. First, because it is just a nice thing to do, second because it is a great, very simple, and inexpensive way to get someone to remember you and your company, (I know a member that still has on his desk a paper weight that he was given many years ago, and guess who he thinks about every time he moves the paper weight) and three, because it is a BNI policy – General Policy No. 8 in fact. But, in truth it's far more than that and here's why.

I really enjoy visiting chapters and watching and listening to a good 10 Minutes. I always learn something about the speaker I didn't know before and most often that member, who has not really been on my radar before, suddenly becomes far more focused in my mind – referrals suddenly seem easier to find. It might be that there is something in their Bio that gets my attention (makes a connection with me), or that by having more time they are able to explain something about their business that wasn't really clear to me before.

However, all this good work can be undone in a second. It gets to the Door Prize and when asked if they have one, the answer is *"Oh. No - I forgot."*

From my point of view, in that moment the whole 10 Minutes is wasted! Anyone can get up and say anything about their business and we trust, until we have proof, that it is true. But, for that moment it is just words. On the other hand a Door Prize is proof of what you think of your fellow members and how professional you are. A member has six weeks to find a door prize – six weeks to think of something that says something great about them – six weeks to wrap it nicely.

Please don't ruin a good (maybe great) 10 Minutes presentation because you couldn't be bothered to get a Door Prize. It says a great deal more about you and your company than you may think.

Note: Chapter Directors please may I suggest that you check with your 10 Minutes speaker as soon as they arrive that they have a Door Prize.

No-one to talk to!

7/9/08

I was with a member recently (they had been in their chapter for a couple of months) and they were saying that they weren't really sure what to do because a few times they had found themselves with no-one to talk to during the open networking part of the meeting. Everyone seemed to be deep in conversation and they didn't feel that they could butt in so they just got a coffee and hoped.

Well, the first thing that struck me was what were the Visitor Hosts doing? At every meeting Visitor Hosts should be looking for people that somehow have ended up on their own – not just visitors but members too (and of course Substitutes). There is nothing worse than being left on your own at any event and all members should look out for people who have become isolated.

Then, of course, there is the Networking Skills workshop. This will not only teach you how to network but also give you tips on how to make yourself feel more comfortable in a room of people you don't know – including how to spot a group that you can easily join.

But, one simple thing that you can try at your next meeting is this: when you have got your coffee, rather than stand around the coffee table hoping that someone might come and find you, instead take your coffee and make your way to the Sign-In desk. Then, when people arrive, welcome them and walk with them to the coffee table – and have something ready to say. Something more than a weather report – maybe something that you have heard on the news about their industry or if there was something in particular that they looking for at the moment. Could you help?

You never know, you might find you really start to enjoy yourself and are never left without someone to talk to again. In short – I suppose I am saying act like a Visitor Host!

Always complaining!

10/9/08

Have you ever come across those people who are always complaining – and you do your best to avoid them?

Well, maybe now it is time to pick and choose those people that you try to hide from because complaints are often referral opportunities.

We are not looking for the mum who says her son doesn't make his bed or our mate at work who thinks that he could run his favourite sports team better than the manager – but what we are looking for are genuine grumbles that could lead to a chance of business.

Let me give you a couple examples: that same mum, over a cup of tea tells you that she just can't keep up with the housework – it's never ending! Is there a cleaner in your chapter? And, your mate at work, you are having a drink one evening after work, and he is moaning about the coming week-end and all the work he has to do. Clear the garden, fix a gate, put back a water pipe that has come loose. Some he doesn't know how to do and others he hasn't got the right tools for, so that means going to the DIY store and wasting more money! Have you a handyman or a gardener in your group?

So, don't switch off when people start to complain and you never know you might start making a lot of people very happy!

Leaflets left behind...

20/9/08

Have you ever been one of the last to leave your meeting and scattered around the tables are the leaflets that a member gave out? I have often – and it's not only been leaflets. Sometimes there have been note pads, invitations to a private view, free tickets to a seminar, all kinds of things.

A few weeks ago I was just leaving a meeting and a member was collecting up their product brochures that had been left behind, so I collected those nearest me and handed them to the member. I guessed only a few could have been taken by the members. They thanked me and I replied, *"No problem"*.

The member then said a funny thing: *"I really meant thank you for taking my brochure"*. I had one amongst my things. We then talked for a few minutes and I have to say that they were pretty disappointed that almost no-one had taken their brochure.

Thinking about it later, what the member said, certainly had a ring of truth about it.

Whenever I am given something at a meeting I take it away with me – not because I am interested necessarily in whatever it might be myself, but because I may be able to pass it on to someone else who is and, more importantly, as I have not been able to read it during the meeting, I can read it later when I can concentrate better and find out something more about the member.

But what the member said that really hit home was two things: first, that obviously the other members weren't really bothered about them or their services and second, that they didn't really feel like putting themselves out for those members during the coming week!

I have to say that I gave out some of my company's pads during my 10 Minutes once and had to collect up a handful afterwards and I must confess that I was not too happy with the members who left them.

So, please take handouts away with you and read them. Not only will it assist you in finding referrals for that member but it may very well increase the number that you receive.

Chapter Directors have you done a good job?

21/9/08

All BNI chapter Leadership Teams change in nine days time. Most will say, *"Has it already been six months?"* as they can't believe how quickly the times flies by and they have so much more they want to do.

But the question is, if you are a Chapter Director, on the 30th September will you have done a good job?

You may run a great meeting, the member numbers are up, as is the referral rate, more members have attended training than ever before, and the meeting room is full by 6.45am each week.

However, have you checked with your Membership Co-ordinator that all is okay? Are they up to date with any control letters that should have gone out, are there any membership committee issues boiling up? Have you checked with your Secretary Treasurer that all is okay with the finances of the chapter, that there aren't any members behind with their meeting fees? And, most importantly, that they will be handing over a clean set of chapter accounts to the next Secretary Treasurer?

Please don't let the new Leadership Team discover on the 1st October what you should know now. Be sure that you can say that you did a good job: in fact, a brilliant job.

Don't make your substitute look silly!

30/9/08

In fact it's not really a case of making your substitute look silly, it's more a case of not making yourself look badly prepared.

It's happened before but what made it stick in my mind recently was the fact that the same thing happened in three different meetings one after the other! The substitute got up and read the script that they had been given and each time had to stop: the first time because something had been added to a typed sheet and the person wasn't sure where the next part was, the second time because the hand-written copy was so bad that they couldn't understand it, and the third time because what they had been given just didn't make sense.

I can even remember cases where the substitute has stood up and said, "... said they would send me something but nothing turned up, so I'll just say what it says on their card".

No, it doesn't make your substitute look silly but it does embarrass them and they do spend a great deal of time apologising.

So, please be kind to the person who is substituting for you and send them a perfect copy of the 60 Seconds that you want them to present for you. And, ask them to read it in advance and come back to you if all is not clear.

Not only will your substitute not mind covering for you again in the future but you will be demonstrating to the group how well organised you are!

Mine's an Aston Martin!

14/10/08

I often liken BNI to a car: in fact in two different ways.

The first, is simply that BNI is a vehicle for 'Word of Mouth' marketing and as with cars there are many such organisations around. It just so happens that, like BNI, Aston Martin is the best! Okay, some of you may disagree and say Ferrari, but I think I make my point! The second way I use the comparison is when people say BNI is not working for them.

I've got my brand new, shiny Aston Martin in Tungsten Silver. The engine is perfect, the interior spotless, it has a full tank of fuel. I'm free to use it exactly as I please. But, say I forget to put any fuel in it and I run out of petrol – do I blame Aston Martin? Or, maybe I miss the odd service and that beautiful engine begins to run rough – do I blame Aston Martin? Maybe, worse still, I'm not too careful with it and I scrape its beautiful bodywork – do I blame Aston Martin? No, no and no! Not ever!

When I'm told that BNI is not working for someone I tell my little story and say that BNI is not to blame. BNI have supplied a brilliant package but as a member you have to supply the fuel, to service it, and give it the care it deserves.

So, before you say that BNI is not working for you, please check to see if you are looking after your investment. Are you making the most of each meeting? Are you doing One2Ones? Have you attended all of the workshops at least once? And finally, have you asked your BNI Director for help?

A Power Team requires four members

28/10/08

Last Friday was the 2008 Members' Day at the London Heathrow Marriott. One of the presentations I found really interesting was given by Andy and Sandra who run BNI Ireland.

The workshop was called 'Does Size Matter?'. Not sure if the title was their idea! But, I went anyway and joined a packed room to hear them talk.

One of their ideas was to grow your chapter by growing your own Power Team (group, circle). Nothing new there, but what was really interesting was their demonstration of the relationships in a team and how they grow.

A Power Team with just one member is nothing more really than just a lonely member. With two members in the Power Team it gives you some-one to wave to across the room. Even with three members in your Power Team you are still just a group of mutually interested individuals. Because three people only have three relationships.

But with four members in your Power Team this is where things suddenly become interesting because now you have six relationships. You really are becoming a Power Team.

And, with seven members in your Power Team you have an amazing 21 relationships! Andy and Sandra call this 'An effective Power Team'

So, if you want more business and to help your chapter grow, think who you can add to your Power Team.

I do!

1/11/08

When a new member joins their BNI chapter, having been accepted by the Membership Committee, they are inducted into the group by the Chapter Director.

This normally requires the new member to join the Chapter Director centre stage to be welcomed into the group and to agree to the BNI Code of Ethics. Chapter Directors and BNI Directors treat this induction in many different ways, from just a straight reading of the code to having a bit of fun: raise your right hand, roll up your left trouser leg.... Just a joke to settle the nerves – I've never seen it done!

Whichever method is chosen, the new member will need to say *"I will"* or *"I do"* in acceptance of the Code of Ethics and this usually results in a few witticisms – *"It's okay, you're not getting married!"* being a favourite.

Well, this week the new member turned the tables on the Chapter Director. The lady concerned was asked to join the Chapter Director at the head of the meeting and as she made her way to the front she slipped a tiara on to her head and produced a bouquet of flowers to hold! All the way through the Code of Ethics she stood and gazed sweetly at the Chapter Director and then said *"I will"* when required.

She brought the house down and without doubt her attitude will make her a great new member of her Chapter.

It's good to talk!

15/11/08

A member asked me recently what they should do because someone in their Chapter had talked about something they themselves did in a 60 Seconds presentation.

Although the service could have been provided by either member, the service concerned was plainly covered by the aggrieved member's category and not by the other member. So, there was a conflict of category.

The member had already talked to the Chapter Director and had been advised to put the matter in writing and hand it into the Membership Co-ordinator for the Membership Committee to consider. Not only was this the correct procedure but also the member's right.

However, I suggested to the member that it might be better to email the Membership Co-ordinator their concerns, but to say that they, the member, would talk to the person concerned first and see what could be done.

My feeling was that once official, something that may have been just an innocent mistake, would develop into something more major with the full committee involved. Whereas a simple chat might resolve the matter without anyone else having to be involved.

The next day the member rang me to say how glad they were that they took my advice. They had met with the other member, who realised as soon as the words were spoken that it was not their area of work and, by talking, had agreed on the boundaries to which they should keep.

But, the best part. They discovered more about each other's businesses and will now be working on a project together!

Chapter Directors – do you know what your new members are being told?

23/11/08

All new members are reminded by their Chapter Directors, once inducted into their chapter, that they need to attend Member Success (Orientation) training within 60 days of joining, otherwise they may be subject to having their category opened by the Membership Committee.

In addition, after attending this workshop the new member will be added to the 10 Minutes speaker list.

But, Chapter Directors, when was the last time that you went to Member Success training? Do you know what your new members are being taught? I believe that it is vitally important for the Chapter Director to know what new members are being told; I also believe that it is as important for the Membership Co-ordinator and Education Co-ordinator to know as well.

So, if you are a Chapter Director, and you have not been to Member Success training within the past year, please may I recommend that you go as soon as possible?

Not only will you be helping your Chapter, you will also be helping those new members, and you never know you might just be reminded of something that you have forgotten.

No cards in the Chapter box!

6/12/08

I have been to a few Chapters recently for the first time and, as usual when the chapter business card box was passed to me, I took one of each card from it. I then tried to put a face to each card I had and the interesting thing was that on each occasion there were at least four members who didn't have a card in the box.

After the meeting I asked these people for their cards and received a mixture of replies. *"Yes of course"* from those that hadn't topped-up the box, to those that had left their cards in the office, and, most surprising, to those that didn't even have a business card!

Upon checking I also discovered that these same members didn't have their business cards represented in the other members' BNI card wallets.

That's just amazing! How many referrals are these members missing out on?

Each week when the business card box is passed round, members flick through the cards taking out those they need, but at the same time they register all the other cards, reinforcing that member in their memory. But even more important, when a member's card wallet is being passed round possible contacts, these missing members' cards are never seen – possible referrals are lost for good.

So, next week when you get to your Chapter, check that you have a really good number of cards in the box and if you don't have any cards, get some this week! But, please don't be tempted to buy those cheap, odd sized 'cards' from the internet. Your business card says a great deal about your business.

As soon as you hand out a cheap business card, it tells your prospect that you are a small company with very little money. It might just make them think twice about using your services!

And, how about this for an idea? If you are the printer in your group, why not see which of your members don't have business cards and then offer them a group deal for a really smart set?

No testimonial!

8/12/08

When you receive a testimonial it's a great feeling, having someone else stand up and tell the whole group how good you and your company are just can't be beaten. It will increase the trust that people have in you and will increase the odds of you receiving even more referrals. But, a testimonial is not a right!

I say this because I have had a couple of members complain to me that they have done work and not been given a testimonial for it. Well, there are a number of reasons why this might be the case.

If the work was for a third party, a testimonial can sometimes be hard to obtain. If the work was for a fellow member, they may think, as I do, that a testimonial should only be given if the work or service was exceptional.

A testimonial should be viewed like feedback. Many business people spend time and money on customer surveys. But in BNI we get this service for free, it's just that we have to work a little harder for the results.

Say a testimonial scores a five (exceptional), then no testimonial could be either a three (good) or a one (poor). The question, is which?

So, if you are wondering why you have not received a testimonial, do a little research and you may just improve both your business and referral rate.

Have you taken your partner to your meeting?

14/12/08

Does your partner, wife, husband, girlfriend, boyfriend, wonder just what you see in your weekly Chapter meetings? Do they look at you with pity? Just can't see what all the fuss is about? And, can't believe, that come rain or shine, every week you are out of bed at 5.30am to go to some strange business meeting where people just help each other?!

Well, I know a great many members whose partners don't get BNI and, if you are in the same position, why not take them to your next meeting?

Why? Because it's amazing how a meeting can completely change their point of view of what you get up to each week. I've seen it happen a number of times. Suddenly they understand what BNI is all about. Seeing it with their own eyes, meeting the other members, shows them what you were never really able to explain.

It's the same as when you are inviting any visitor – you just can't do justice to a great meeting in simple words.

I was at a chapter recently where a member's wife was subbing for her husband. She opened with, *"I don't think much of these meetings"*, and basically told us that she thought BNI was pretty much a waste of time, but her husband needed her to be there so here she was. Not a great start to the morning I can tell you and I hoped that the visitors in the room didn't meet her! After the meeting she came up to me, a smile all over her face. She said that she had been wrong and had completely changed her mind. Everyone had made her feel so welcome and she just hadn't reliaised what a great group of people the members were.

But, do you want to know the other thing that happens? They pass referrals! I heard one lady whisper to her husband, *"...you didn't tell me about that lovely lady who does head massage, with candles and music ..."*

And, if you are really lucky, having met the members and listened to what they do, your partner will start to find referrals.

So, your fellow members will be more than happy and with luck you will have an extra referral source for good!

Secret Santa

24/12/08

At one of the Chapters I visited this week, instead of the normal 10 Minutes speaker, they had a Chapter Secret Santa. The Events Co-ordinator had arranged it: members pulling a name of another member out of a hat of who they would buy a present for. All the presents were beautifully wrapped and given out by each member going to the pile of presents, one at a time, and randomly picking one to give. Everyone then waited until all the presents were distributed before opening. Once unwrapped each member informed the group of what they had received.

This was the fascinating part, as some members had looked upon the idea as a bit of fun, while others has taken it more seriously. The presents ranged from chocolates and bottles of wine, to joke books and books that were well-suited to the member, to things that matched personality: one member received a beard trimmer, he has a bushy beard; another a recorder, he is a musician; part of another member's present was a money box for a millionaire: the member talks about how to become a millionaire. Some presents were very interesting: one member received a fire-extin-guisher; another a posing-pouch!

It was a brilliant event and with every member taking part wonderful for the chapter – a great way to start Christmas.

But, what was very fascinating was that you could tell which members really knew the member that they had bought a present for and those who did not. And, I couldn't help thinking that some more One2Ones would help those particular members to get to know each other better and, by doing so, increase their chances of a referral from one another.

Twenty business cards

29/12/08

I failed!

For a recent Regional Director training event we were asked to bring along the business cards of our top twenty business contacts. But, as I didn't know who was going to attend the workshop I decided that I wouldn't. After all, you have to know, like, and trust people before you share your most important contacts with them.

But it was a test: a request to prove a point. And, I failed.

I was attending a workshop, held by my Area Director, and attended by other Regional Directors. Whilst I may have not known them all, they were all my equal – all good BNI members. And yet, I would not even risk taking a pocket full of my contacts' business cards with me to the training.

Now, what did this prove? Well, as members we expect new members, in fact all members, to share their contacts with us. But, why should they if we have made no effort to get to know them? If we have given them no reason to like us or trust us.

As members we spend a great deal of time telling our fellow members what we do and how they can best find us referrals. But, how much time do we spend giving our fellow members good reasons as to why they should share their best contacts with us?

It is often said that people buy from people. Members refer to people. Are you giving your fellow chapter members a good reason to find you referrals?

Choose what your Chapter looks like!

4/1/09

I sometimes hear members say that their chapter does not have the right members in it: too many of one thing, not enough of another, that their Power Group is too small. And I always suggest the same thing .... Do something about it!

Members are the result of people invited. And, any member can influence the make-up of their chapter by simply inviting the type of people that they want as members.

So, if you want more members in your Power Team, invite only people that make up your team. If you want more trades people, only invite those types of businesses. If you want more women in your group, only invite women. The choice is yours.

But you have to do it. You have to invite people. Don't leave it to someone else because they will invite whom they want, not whom you want.

Your Chapter may not look the way you want it because you haven't invited anyone who has become a member. Invite and keep inviting, and you never know, in a few months time your Chapter may just look the way you would like it to.

Absence makes the heart grow fonder!

8/1/09

It may in love, but it certainly won't in your Chapter!

I've never understood why people miss business meetings, and your BNI meeting is a business meeting. After all, you have made a commitment. Why wouldn't you turn up? What are you saying about the people that you are about to meet? That you don't care about them? That they are not important?

Now, I know that there are emergencies, and that sometimes accidents happen, but I really find it hard to believe that a member who really cares about their fellow members can reach three or more absences.

But that's me, and what I think doesn't really matter, but what does matter is the effect that an absence has on the member.

Now, some of you might be thinking what effect can it possibly have, other than a tick in the absence column of the PALMS report. Well, here's the answer.

I should have said answers, as there are many consequences to missing your Chapter meeting.

The most immediate effect is that being absent reduces the chances of you receiving any referrals the following week. Why? Because you didn't educate the Chapter on what you were looking for. And, as you weren't there, why should they think about you that week? Whereas a substitute, although not as good as the member, will continue the education process and your visibility in the group and, in doing so, improves the chances of more referrals the next week.

But, there is far more to it than that. An absence, especially more than one, has a much greater effect on the success of your membership than you might imagine. You not only miss the opportunity to give your 60 Seconds, but, more importantly, you don't hear the 60 Seconds of your fellow members. This results in you giving fewer referrals, and yes, in receiving referrals! Givers Gain.

Then, we have the fact that you have missed a member's 10 Minutes presentation. How much easier would it be to find referrals for that member if you had been there? Then again, how do you feel when members miss your 10 Minutes slot?

And, what about the open-networking before and after the meeting? Building trust, finding out how you can help people, and letting them know how they can help you.

None of us would miss a business meeting unless it was a real emergency; so, think about your BNI meeting for what it really is. A business meeting!

What are your friends reading?

10/1/09

Often the reason that members find it difficult to find referrals is because they don't know how to ask for them. Well, not ask for exactly, but start a conversation about a member in their Chapter. They don't have any 'openers'. A phrase, something to start the conversation with, that will lead to a member being discussed.

Well, how about this for an idea? I was attending a Referral Skills workshop where members were being asked to share with the group ways of finding referrals that had been successful for them. And I thought the following was a great idea.

Next time you go to a friend's home, in fact any home, have a look at what magazines are on the coffee table, on the kitchen units, on a desk, or by the side of the sofa. Is the magazine open at a particular page? That's your 'opener'!

How easy would it be to motion to the magazine and say *"Gardens, hard work aren't they? Thinking of a change?"* And, off you go. Or, how about if a bathroom magazine is open at a page showing a beautiful fully tiled bathroom, you could say something like *"Is that what your new bathroom is going to look like? I tried tiling. Never again!"* And, once again you are into a conversation, where you might be able to introduce your plumber, electrician, carpenter, plasterer, maybe all of them. They might even need a builder, or even a mortgage broker to raise the funds for the job.

But, the most important thing is your 'opener'. After that there is no telling where the conversation will lead, or how many referrals you might be able to make. Happy reading!

Pick up your visitor!

26/1/09

Have you ever been let down by a visitor? You rang them the day before your meeting to confirm that all was okay and then the next morning they didn't show. I don't know about you but I have been.....more than once.

So, now, whenever possible, I offer to pick up and bring my visitors to my Chapter meetings. It has made a big difference with the number of my visitors that attend. I bet they turn over in bed when the alarm goes, and instead of pushing the snooze button for another ten minutes (and then of course it gets too late), they think instead, 'That really nice BNI bloke will be here in a minute. Better get going!'

Don't know if it is just the thought of this offer, but even those that don't accept my kind offer tend to arrive!

But, do you know what else I have discovered by doing this? My relationship with the visitor starts in the car, in fact before that, as I have offered to take them to the meeting. In the car we have to talk, it's almost a One2One, on top of which I can explain and put them at ease about the meeting that they are about to walk into.

I have found it a great method. Why not give it a try?

Beat that!

2/2/09

Platinum Chapter member Barry Sutton took off his gloves today and laid down a challenge to his fellow members. Most of the country may have been covered in snow but that wasn't going to stop Barry having a bit of fun and gaining an advantage where he could! Late in the afternoon he sent an email to his Chapter which said: *"OK Guys. Every ten years or so we get some snowfall and it's customary to have a snowman competition. Here is my entry. Beat that!"*

So, did any other Chapters have a snowman competition or maybe even a snowball fight? It's these kinds of things that help you get to know each other and what I've learnt today is that, if I want to beat Barry, next time it snows I'm going to have to get up early!

Hope you weren't unlucky enough to be stuck in it somewhere but had some fun in the snow.

BNI New Zealand

8/2/09

One of the things that has surprised me about my blog is the type of person who reads it. Or rather, those that think my blog is of value. Let's face it anyone could read it!

And I have to say that it is pretty good when someone leaves a comment saying that it's a worthwhile read, especially when it is someone like Graham Southwell, the National Director of New Zealand.

Having been spotted by Graham I decided to subscribe to the Official Blog of BNI New Zealand and now I receive an alert every time something new is posted.

Their post on how to better convert visitors to members caught my eye so I thought that I would share it:
http://bniblog.co.nz/bni/bni-workshops/how-to-convert-visitors-into-members/

Hope the post gives you some ideas. See what Graham Southwell said:
https://www.blogger.com/comment.g?blogID=3403756724341668639&postID=4825241438186385778

Ten business cards

16/2/09

I was helping my Area Director present the One2One Relationship Skills Workshop this week. In one of the open discussion parts of the workshop ideas were being exchanged on how to best maximise the opportunities for the other person.

Something my Area Director suggested, as it is what she does, is ask the member she is having the One2One with for ten business cards. Once back in her office, she attaches each card around her computer screen with some Bluetack. In this way, when emailing and on the telephone, she has a ready reminder of the person that she is looking to help.

Then, when an opening arises to recommend the member, she has all their necessary information to hand. And the best part? Until she has been able to give out all ten cards she does not have another One2One. She is completely focused on that one member. What a great idea!

Can another BNI member ever be a good substitute?

19/2/09

A survey was done some time ago where members were asked *"If a member of your chapter could not attend a meeting, who would you like to see in their chair as a sub?"*

I'm not going to run through the Top 10 now, but at number seven, was *"Anyone…with a heartbeat".* And, at number eight, was another BNI member.

So, I guess you could say that the answer to my question was – No!

However, we had a BNI member from another Chapter sub at our Chapter last week. Sadly nothing unusual in that, apart from the fact that she didn't present her business, as she clashed with one of our members – so, she didn't do a 60 Seconds. In fact she didn't really talk about her business much at all and she didn't even pass around her business cards. She was subbing for the right reason – giving to a friend.

And it reminded me of an email that I had received some time last year. In short, the email said that a member of a Chapter was looking for a sub for a very good friend of theirs, only that they themselves could not sub for the friend, because they clashed with someone in the chapter.

Now my question is, what sort of friend were they? And, I would have to say – Not a friend at all.

So, if you are asked to sub in the future, make sure that you are not just the 'soft' option and then ask yourself before saying yes, *"Would I still say yes if I couldn't present my business?"*

The really great thing about the BNI member that subbed at our meeting last week, was that when I left she was having a One2One with the person she clashed with.

Two members that both understand what BNI is all about.

Brilliant BNI song!

23/2/09

I've just been told about a BNI Song on YouTube by Richard Swan – and just watched it. It's a must see, just click below.

http://www.youtube.com/watch?v=UPZetC8jPhY

A 'giving' 10 Minutes

25/2/09

At a recent Chapter visit I was lucky enough to experience one of the best 10 Minutes presentations I have ever seen. It wasn't great because of the props used – there weren't any – nor because the member was an amazing performer, nor because of an eye-catching PowerPoint slide show, and not even because the content was stunning, but because of its simplicity and what was given.

The presentation was delivered in three sections and it was the middle part that really got my attention. The member talked about his customers and what type of business sector they were in. He then told us that he had been through his current client base and had 305 active accounts. At this point he turned over to a new flip chart sheet and on it was a list of his customers by sector. He then asked everyone to study the names and if they wanted introductions into any of them he would do his best for them.

What an offer!

I have to say that I was more than a little impressed. At a time when he could have been doing his utmost to educate the Chapter on how to find him referrals he was using his time to help his fellow members.

A real ten out of ten 10 Minutes!

Is your meeting like a great party?

8/3/09

And, no I don't mean with lots of champagne, loud music and dancing!

I'm sure that like me, sometime in your life, you have been invited to a party that, to be honest, wasn't that great. For some reason the party just didn't get going; there was music, more than enough to drink, and friends in the room. But there was no spark, no feeling of fun, so you had a drink, grabbed a plate full of food, smiled at a few people and tried to have a good time. All the time wondering how soon it would be polite to make your excuses and leave.

On the other hand (I hope), we have all been to really fantastic parties, where as soon as you walk in the room you just know that you are going to have a good time. Funny thing is that if you think about it there is nothing different about the structure of the party: music, drink, food and people. And yet it's totally different and the thought of leaving doesn't even cross your mind. You love the music, dance the night away, laugh, and just can't stop talking. Until in the end your host has to push you out of their door and promises to have another party soon.

That is what our Chapter meetings need to feel like. When visitors, and members, come to our meetings do they wish they hadn't come or do they feel as if the meeting is over almost as soon as they are welcomed into the room?

Every BNI meeting has the same structure – our twenty point agenda – so it is up to us to make our meetings feel like that great party. Make sure that you are part of the energy in the room by getting to your meetings early and acting like the perfect host. I think you will be surprised at the difference that it will make to your chapter.

Chapter Director blown away!

13/3/09

My business, Imperial Printers, had a stand at the first Richmond Networking Expo09 on Thursday, as in fact did my BNI Chapter – Business Class.

The event was sponsored by the Best of Richmond and held at the Harlequins' Rugby ground and was a great success. It was also the first time that we had been an exhibitor at an event and we too had a brilliant time, although I have to say that standing for seven hours is pretty hard on the feet!

Anyway, this morning, in the cold light of day, things are still buzzing at BNI Business Class and the feedback from the members is just amazing.

And, as for our Chapter Director, well he is just totally 'blown away' by the whole thing. Below is an email he sent me about the event, which I think says it all.

The definition of giving:

There is an old adage in football: teams that drink together, win together. I suppose it means that if your teammates are also your friends you will make that extra effort for them.

There can be no doubt that the people in our Chapter are friends.

Yesterday, at the Best of Richmond Expo, BNI had a stand and BNI Business Class had our own separate stand.

All our members were in evidence from 3pm. This included setting up what was an innovative, attractive and welcoming stand. It told those who attended the Expo that, all the talk of gloom is just that, talk, because at Business Class, business is done and business is fun.

The members then spent the rest of the Expo talking to potential visitors about how great our Chapter is.

None of them were selling their own products, instead they were each working to get business for their fellow members. And the result? A stampede of people desperate to join our Chapter.

And when I left the show late into the evening, what were the remaining members doing?

Drinking together!

Two signs of a great Chapter!

22/3/09

Obviously there are many things that make a great Chapter and, even if I came up with a Top 10 list, someone else would have their own opinion.

For example, it could be the amount of business that a Chapter has been thanked for in the 'Thank you for the business' (Show me the Money) box, it could be the number of referrals passed, the fact that most members have been to all of the Workshops, or that every week they have two or more visitors, or it could be that their chapter has 44 members, or maybe that they have wonderful social events.

In truth I suspect that it will be a combination of all of these things and more.

But, if you want two, easy to spot signs of a great Chapter just count the number of members at the meeting by 6.30am and again at 9.00am. Great Chapters are buzzing by 6.30am and are still full at 9.00am.

So, have a quick count of the members at your next meeting. If more than 60% of your fellow members are present then you might just have yourself a great Chapter.

Why stand up?

29/3/09

A question you often hear from new members in BNI is – Why do I have to stand when I am talking?

I've also seen many visitors stay sitting when it is their turn to speak, lots of frantic gesturing from the members trying to get a person to stand and, most often, a request from the Chapter Director for someone to stand, this being followed by an uneasy or embarrassed rise by the person concerned from their chair.

So, why do we stand when talking?

Well, I guess the easy answer is that it is more businesslike. But, in truth there are far more important reasons than that and they all add up to just one thing. More business!

When we stand to talk we naturally speak louder, we can be seen and everyone's attention is focused on us. Our words are clearer and more easily heard, which means that our presentation is far more effective. I hope that you will agree that it's not too hard to connect a more effective presentation to gaining more business.

And don't rush when you do stand to speak. Only start talking once you are standing and finish talking before you sit down again. I miss so much of members' 60 Seconds who start talking the moment they start to rise from their seats and trail off as they sit again at the end.

Practise what you preach!

4/4/09

Credibility and personal branding are so important in your Chapter and I believe that a great many members just don't understand how important these two things are.

I have a great book called the Perfect Portfolio and in it, amongst other things, the author suggests that you need to open with a 'Bang' and close with a 'Bang', but more important than that, you will only sell what is in your portfolio. In my case as a printer, these is no point going out selling colour leaflets if my portfolio is full of 2-colour letterheads. Things just don't stack up.

And, it is exactly the same in your BNI Chapter. Only in your Chapter you and your company are your portfolio. I will give you some examples to explain.

We once had a web designer join our Chapter, only to discover a short time later that they didn't have a web site themselves. Guess what that did to their credibility? How hard do you think it was to refer a web designer who didn't have a web site?

Can I add here that if you are a web designer and you look after your Chapter's web site, make sure that the Chapter site is always up to date, as if it's not, it will hurt your credibility.

If you are a copywriter your 60 Seconds need to be perfect, every word in exactly the right place and every 60 Seconds exactly that – 60 Seconds.

On the other hand, if you are a Business Coach who says that you can help companies find more business and increase sales, then you must have business yourself. A great way of also showing how good you are at gaining people new business is to be the top visitor bringer to your Chapter.

Then of course you have the Personal Coach – they listen, consider, and help. What do you think it says about that coach if throughout the meeting they are constantly interrupting and not understanding what is being said?

I think that by now you are probably getting the picture – that you have to be what you are selling. You have to look the part. If you are expecting to sell an expensive service you really can't hand out a cheap looking business card you got off the web - you want someone to give you thousands of pounds but can only afford £20 for business cards. Again it doesn't add up.

So, credibility, it's built on everything you do in your Chapter, everything you say, everything you show.

If you are not getting the number of referrals that you think you should, may I suggest that you find a member that you can trust to tell you the truth and ask if your credibiltiy and branding match up to what you are selling. And, if not, how you could improve things. If you can increase your credibility your referrals will follow suit.

Have you hit Tesco?

10/4/09

One thing I often hear in Chapters is that members have no time to look for visitors.

I'm not going to go into how business people don't have time to find new business, but what I will say is that finding visitors need take no time at all. Well, very little!

Most of us shop these days, and whether it's Tesco, or any other super-market, or in fact just about any DIY store, people to invite are just sitting there right in front of us at the checkout.

If you haven't done so before, have a look at the wall behind the tills: you will find a large business card holder full of cards of companies looking for business. The companies that advertise there are spending a great deal of money to have their cards on display. They are looking for business.

And, that's the key: they are looking for more business. That's all a visitor is, someone who is looking for more work, nothing more.

So, next time you are out shopping, look for those business cards and make your visitor inviting easy.

Do you know what fellow members' partners do?

18/4/09

I was chatting to a very successful 12 year member recently at a Workshop and in the course of our conversation I asked him if he had any tips on increasing the amount of business I received from my Chapter. And he asked me if I knew what all my fellow members' partners did.

A little embarrassed, I had to admit that I didn't; worse still, that there were some members in my Chapter whom I didn't even know if they had a partner.

He explained that during his 12 years as a member that he had discovered that the One2One was the most important thing that he did.

He had regular One2Ones with all of the members of his Chapter and that he took an interest in everything that they and their family did.

This had not only gained him a number of really good friends but over the years a great deal of business. Why? Because a great many members' partners work, and, on more than one occasion, have turned out to be just the contact he needed.

So, I have the same question for you. Do you know what your fellow members' partners do? If not, you could be missing out on some really valuable business.

Use your ears!

22/4/09

Want more business from your fellow members? Then use your ears: listen and remember.

It doesn't matter if it's during open networking, during the meeting, at a social, or even if 'by accident' you hear other members talking. Use your ears!

How many times have you heard a member mention in the course of a conversation a company's name? The name comes and goes and more often than not you think nothing of it. You might nod, or even say *"Wow! What a great company to work for"*, but five minutes later the company name is forgotten.

What if you remembered that company? What if that company would be a great contact for you? You can't interrupt, especially if you are listening to someone else's conversation, and say *"Hey, that would be a great contact for me!"* but what you can do is remember the name and in the future, during a One2One, ask about the company. Ask how the member got the business in the first place and how good their relationship was. And, if it seems right, would the member be prepared to give you a personal introduction?

Your fellow members often don't realise which of their contacts you might be interested in, but if asked are only too willing to help you gain business.

So, use your ears and get more business. Oh, a little tip – always carry a small notebook. You never know when you might need it!

12th Annual BNI European Conference – Amsterdam

26/4/09

My third conference and the best so far. My first, in Southampton is just a dull memory. All I can remember is a team building game and that Frank De Raffele was brilliant: I thought about BNI the same way he did.

Dublin was better, I knew the ropes now, was on one of the Steering Committees for the year, there was a great presentation by Andrew Hall and I was sitting next to one of the lovely ladies from BNI Head Office at the Awards Dinner.

I know I've only just arrived back, so everything is fresh in my mind, but Amsterdam was without doubt the best!

We started, even before the conference started, at 7.30am Friday morning with a London North West group One2One with Sandra and Andy Hart. I would have been happy to have gone home after breakfast with the advice they gave, but then the conference was opened by Frank De Raffele. What a great way to set the tone for the next two days! My personal highlight of the morning was choosing to attend the Breakout Session by Mike Holman which was straight talking and full of sound practical advice.

In the afternoon was an hour of 10 Minutes presentations: a very thought-provoking one by Peter Hemmen (Netherlands), based on Roger Bannister's 4 minute mile, about changing your mindset, a great One2One plan from Samantha Rathling (Ireland South & West) which provides a referral every time, but the best in my mind was a sensational 10 Minutes by Kathleen Waller (London North West) on how to present an outstanding 10 Minutes. It had everything – other than the use of props!

Saturday opened with the National Directors' Report, this year hosted by Charlie Lawson and Tim Cook, and included a little Directors Quiz. I'm glad to report that I scored in the top 20%! This was followed by another set of Breakout Sessions and, judging by the feedback at the end of the conference, provided the outstanding moment of the whole two days! This was a truly motivating and, for some, life changing, session by Dinah Liversidge, entitled 'Building Your Business by Building Your Credibility'. A spontaneous standing ovation and queue of people wanting to shake her hand said all that was needed to be said.

But still we had the afternoon to come, and for me, overall, this provided my own personal highlight. Rob Brown – what a show! – 'Stand Up and Stand Out'. If I just took 10% of what he showed us and put it into action, it would change me and my business for the better.

Again this one session would have made the conference so much more than just worthwhile; in a way it was my own 'life changing' moment.

Well, what was left to come? The Black Tie Awards Dinner. Would we get an award this year? Yes we did: an award for opening new chapters. And I was happy to have been able to help London North West win it by launching the Iolanthe chapter during the year. But there was still more to come! After the awards and before the serious part of the evening started, the dancing, Gillian and Martin Lawson had a very special announcement to make. They were retiring with immediate effect, official date 1st May, and Charlie Lawson and Tim Cook were taking over as Joint National Directors.

What a moment when Martin thanked Gillian for all she had done over the last thirteen years, watched by all of their children who had joined us for the occasion.

And the saddest part of the two days? Being caught by Sandra Hart at midnight, while everyone else was dancing, checking my BNI emails!

Know your 10 Minutes speaker!

7/5/09

Something that really impressed me at the recent BNI Directors' Conference in Amsterdam was the way in which David O'Dell introduced the speakers. He had been given a biography on the person that he was to introduce, but instead used his own personal knowledge of the speaker, gained from the relationship he had with them, to make the introduction. Not only did it build his own credibility but it gave a far better and warmer introduction to the person he was introducing. It was genuine and really demonstrated his liking and trust of the person concerned and really started the whole presentation in a very positive way.

This was so much better than the often badly read, married to so and so, children none, pets none, home town, Oh, can't read that but I think it says they were there for eleven years, and so it goes on. What does that say about the person and what you think about them?

So, Secretary/Treasurers how about this for an idea? If you don't already know the 10 Minutes speaker really well, how about having a One2One with them a couple of weeks before they are due to speak? Not only will you be able to give them a much better introduction, but you will be building your own credibility, and increasing the number of referrals you pass between each other.

But I suggest that it might be worth asking the speaker if they mind you doing your own introduction of them just in case there is something in their biography that they really want the group to know.

Overall this is what they call a Win, Win, Win situation!

What are you talking about at 6.30am?

11/5/09

Most good BNI members arrive at around 6.30am for their weekly Chapter meeting, leaving at just after 8.30am to continue their day's work.

The open networking part of the meeting from 6.30am until 7.10am, when the formal part of the meeting starts, therefore represents around 35% of the total meeting time.

Now, I have a question for you. Would you spend 35% of your working week talking about sport, or what you did last night? Well that is exactly what some members do at their BNI meeting during the open networking part of the meeting.

Now I'm not suggesting that the whole of the time from the moment you arrive at your meeting until the time that you sit down for the formal part of the meeting should be all work. But, should you be spending all of that time on casual chit-chat? How much work would you get done during your normal working week if you spent 35% just talking about the weather?

So, make the most of the open networking part of your weekly meeting.

Have a plan: of course catch up on last night's football scores with your best mate, that's all part of building a great relationship, but also use the time to find out how you can help your fellow members and also to let them know how they can help you.

18/5/09

Recently, my Area Director was telling me about a Chapter visit she had made, and in particular about the 60 Seconds she had listened to. Or, to be more precise, one she had not heard.

She had turned to the member beside her and whispered, *"I didn't hear anything they said!"* And the member replied that in over a year that they hadn't heard anything either!

I won't tell you anything else of the story, other than to say that if there is someone in your Chapter that you can't hear, please be a good friend and let them know.

However, it got me thinking. Does any of us really know what our fellow members think of our 60 Seconds? Not just can they hear us, but do we educate them? Is our message clear? Do they know what we are looking for? Are they crystal clear about exactly what we do?

We might think that we are doing a great job, but, especially if referrals are low, do our fellow members agree?

So, I have a couple of ideas that you might like to try. The first is easy. Every time that you have a One2One make it one of your questions. Ask if your 60 Seconds are providing the right kind of information to help find you referrals.

The second idea is more difficult to do and may result in you opening yourself up to some harsh truths, but may well result in some great business in the future. Find someone in the chapter whom you really trust and whom you know will be objective and ask them to give you some real feedback on your 60 Seconds – warts and all.

If they agree, don't take what they say personally. You asked for their help! Consider their observations and suggestions, and, if you agree, change your 60 Seconds accordingly. And then ask them for their feedback again. Oh, and why not ask them if they would like some feedback on their 60 Seconds?

Just out of interest – who does your printing?

1/6/09

No, I'm not asking for a referral for my company Imperial Printers but it's a great line to use when looking for referrals for someone in your Chapter. Of course you may have to change the *"Who does your printing?"* part, if you don't have a printer in your Chapter!

But what a great line and it is so easy to use. I can imagine myself as Columbo (I'm watching the re-runs, only joking), turning as I am about to leave a meeting and asking that 'killer' question, *"Just out of interest – who does your lawn-cutting?"* It works with just about any type of business. *"Who does your payroll?"*, *"Who services your car?"*, *"Who does your book-keeping?"*

Then, depending on the answer, you have the perfect start to a conversation that may just lead to a referral. Ask your contact if they are happy with the service that they are getting from their current supplier. Would they be happy to speak to a good friend of yours that is looking for more business and that you can recommend.

Or, you may get lucky and they say, *"Why? Do you know someone? I really need to contact someone now."*

So, why not give it a try this week. Pick someone in your chapter that you would like to find a referral for and every time you leave a meeting this week, or are about to end a telephone conversation, ask *"Just out of interest – who does your xxxxxxx?"*

Have you let anyone down recently?

3/6/09

Trust is a major factor when it comes to people referring you. Let's face it, however good you think a member's service is, would you easily recommend them if you couldn't completely trust them?

I guess the answer is probably no – certainly I know that I would think twice.

It's really important that we don't raise people's hopes by making a promise only to dash them by breaking that promise. It wrecks our credibility and therefore any trust that person has in us.

Now I am not talking big events here; it's the build up of those small broken promises that do the real damage. Have you ever said to someone, *"I'll call you in the morning"*, and not done so? Or, *"I'll pop it in the post"*, and forgotten? Maybe, *"How about coffee on Thursday?"* and totally forgotten about it. Even, set a date for a meeting, *"No fail"* you said, and then changed it.

The list is endless, but each is a promise broken. Sooner or later people will stop believing you and with that goes your credibility. And, after that goes the trust a person had in you.

The result of all this is fewer referrals.

A member asked me recently how they could improve their image within the chapter, get more referrals, and my answer was easy. Keep your promises I advised, as only that very week someone else from the Chapter had complained that they had stayed in all morning waiting for a promised phone call from this member!

Regional Director caught on film!

13/6/09

I was invited to observe at a special presentation skills workshop organised by Anthony Wood, photographer, of the Harlequin chapter, for eight of his fellow members where they would each be filmed and then given feedback on their 60 Seconds.

After they had all had the opportunity to present, it was suggested that I might like a turn as a Regional Director. This was one of those moments! – I had to have a 60 Seconds ready to give.

You can see the result by going on the link:
http://www.youtube.com/watch?v=qAU6zSs2mmE

Focus on your credibility not selling

14/6/09

I was reading SuccessNet Online recently and came across an article in the 'My BNI Story' section which had the title 'The $3M Dollar Deal'. Well, I had to have a look! Wouldn't you? It was only a very short piece and, in fact, these eight words were all that were really needed: 'I focused on building credibility instead of selling'.

Something that a great many BNI members forget is that BNI is not about selling. Selling, if you listen carefully, is seldom mentioned but, on the other hand, Know, Like and Trust are always talked about. And what do Know, Like and Trust all add up to, other than your credibility?

So, if you would like to improve the value of the referrals that you receive, I suggest that you take the advice of Connie Rankin and concentrate on your credibility rather than just selling. The $3M Dollar Deal: http://successnet.czcommunity.com/my-bni-story/the-3m-dollar-deal/2900/

Hogarth Rocks!

20/6/09

Thursday 18th June 2009, the London Rowing Club in Putney and the debut performance of the Hogarth Hogs (maybe their first and their last!).

The Hogarth Chapter of BNI (Chiswick) was the first Chapter in England to take on six new members in the recent Power Team drive. To date they have taken on over ten new members as a result of their efforts and to celebrate they decided to use some of their prize money to have a party as a reward for all of their hard work and also to welcome the new members into the Chapter.

On arrival members were greeted with a glass of Champagne on the balcony of the club overlooking the Thames and rowers below. Then it was down to a little work!

Speed One2Ones. New members being paired with the more long term members, each pairing being given three minutes to discover things about each other, until everyone had had a chance to introduce themselves to everyone else. Well, that was the plan – I think it got a little lost somwhere!

One thing that I discovered was that Yvonne Arzt, the Chapter's Membership Co-ordinator and Interior Designer, had worked in Israel on a large project.

We then sat down to an excellent three course dinner and I was lucky enough to sit with Alex Hutchings (Plumbing & Heating), as during the meal we discovered that not only did we have a part of the country in common, but that we both have a passion for cooking and, what's more, similar dishes.

Then, just before the sweet was served, we were given a taster of what was to come: Norwegian Wood, a duet by Yvonne Arzt and Etienne Baird, accompanied by Will Cheng on guitar.

So, after coffee we were given our instructions to come close to the stage, standing only, after all *"This is a rock concert!"*

The Hogarth Hogs opened with 'I saw Her Standing There' (Beatles), included a rousing rendition of Johnny Be Goode, with some very passionate vocals by Jonathan Hughes (Secretary/Treasurer), and ended with 'Don't Look Back in Anger' (Oasis). In between were some superb guitar solos by Will Cheng and Alan Macdonald (Chapter Director), very tidy drumming from Colin Woodley, all backed up by Roger Severn on bass.

Sadly, there was to be no encore as the band had only learnt just enough songs for their performance during their two rehearsals.

As we once again stood on the balcony, this time watching the tide rise, the talk was all about when the Hogarth Hogs might play again and if Ashley Winston (Car Finder) would have to move his Rolls Royce before the tyres got wet!

A great evening and one that I was very happy to have been invited to. What's more, I can see the headlines now – Hogs Rock!

Hogarth Hogs are:
Alan Macdonald (guitar)
Will Cheng (guitar),
Roger Severn (bass)
Colin Woodley (drums)
Jonathan Hughes, Etienne Baird
and Yvonne Arzt (vocals)
Photography: Philip Coulson

Did you sign in at training?

28/6/09

Just lately I have had a number of members tell me that the training report on BNI Net is wrong with regard to the number of Workshops that they have attended. Any record can only be as accurate as the information that has been supplied, and I think that this is where the workshop booking-in system and therefore record keeping sometimes can break down.

I have been to a number of Workshops recently, both as a member, and Regional Director, and I have noticed that not all members sign in.

On occasion this is because there is a queue at the booking-in desk and the member has got side-tracked, at other times it's just because they don't even attempt to sign in.

Furthermore, at a recent Workshop that I was helping at, I counted the number of people in the room against those that had signed in. The list was two names short, but despite asking the members in the room to check that they were signed in during the coffee break, no-one did (I even added that their attendance at the Workshop would not be recorded if they were not signed in).

Then this week I queried with a member I knew had been at a Workshop, a few days earlier, why she was not on the list of attendees that I had received from BNI Head Office, and she said that people were just sitting down when she arrived, so she just took her place and forgot to sign in later.

So, please may I suggest that if you want to ensure that your training record on BNI Net is correct – REMEMBER TO SIGN IN.

How well do you know your referral?

9/7/09

Most of us when given a referral thank the member who gave it to us, check what it is about, confirm the contact details, and then off we go.

We then contact the person concerned, say who introduced us, and talk about the referral, hoping that this will lead to a meeting and then the opportunity to do some business. And, with a good referral this is exactly what happens.

But, how about this for an idea? Tim Cook, one of the National Directors of UK and Ireland, suggested the following as a great idea for increasing the chances of turning a referral, into a valuable piece of business. His idea is really simple, but I wonder how many of us have had the same idea?

Before you contact the person referred, go back to the member who gave you the referral and ask for some background information on the person. Not too much, just enough to give you a better chance of making a connection. After all BNI is all about liking and trusting each other and building relationships. So why not get some additional facts that might help you bond more quickly with the person referred?

So, if you want to increase your conversion rate of referrals into actual business why not give Tim's idea a try?

Do you wear blinkers at your BNI meeting?

16/7/09

It often happens at networking events, but it should never happen at a BNI meeting. And yet it did this week!

A new member of a group was left on their own. I was busy sorting out some papers for the meeting and watched as she stood not knowing who to talk to; everyone seemed so deep in private conversations.

Finally, I was able to join her and ask how she was, could I introduce her to someone? But she said that she had tried to join in a conversation or two but no one seemed that interested.

To say I was stunned is something of an understatement!

My first thought was what were the Visitor Hosts doing? Having scanned the room I could see that they were all busy, although not with new visitors or visiting substitutes. I then looked for the Leadership Team and they to all seemed to be doing something. And lastly, I looked at the other members; they too seemed busy, deep in conversation with each other or just waiting for a coffee.

Neglecting a visitor or not, can often be the difference between that visitor wanting to join your Chapter or not. So, whether you are a Visitor Host, Leadership Team member, or a member, please never leave anyone on their own.

Take your blinkers off and make sure you watch out for anyone left on their own. Not just visitors, but also substitutes and new members. On occasion even established members can't find a conversation to join.

Imagine how you would feel left on your own in a room full of people and take action!

Have you had a better offer?

22/7/09

I've heard of a similar thing happening twice recently and I have to say it worries me, not only from a BNI point of view, but also from a purely business perspective.

The first occasion was when a person rang to confirm an appointment that had been made some weeks earlier, only to be told by the company concerned that they were just about to call them, to let them know that they couldn't make the meeting because something urgent had come up.

The second example was, in fact, even worse: the company concerned rang the customer the day before they were due to carry out the work, to let them know that they wouldn't be coming because they had secured a more profitable job!

Business-wise both of these instances are very short sighted, but telling a prospective client that you are taking on a more profitable job than theirs is, well, just unbelievable.

Overall, to my mind any way, it's just bad business. But in BNI terms it could mean death!

Neither of the members concerned is ever likely to refer these companies again. Having been told about these two companies I too would not refer them. So, think of the potential business that has already been lost.

On top of this, one of the companies concerned was being tested. A large contract was due to be placed. Obviously they didn't get it.

Now you may be asking why I wouldn't refer these companies in the future, as obviously from time to time things go wrong. And, of course, you are right.

But the point is this. Yes, things do go wrong on occasion, but under normal circumstances it's your credibility and reputation that is on the line. It's your customer to lose and so your choice.

But in BNI, it's my reputation and credibility as well as yours that are at stake. Can I really recommend someone that I know could let down my best customer at the last moment? I don't think so, do you? And, what is more, it's not even just my credibility that is at stake, it's the whole Chapter's, since if my judgement is proved to be unsafe, I will never be trusted again by my contact.

So, if you really want to build your credibility in your chapter never let down someone that has been referred to you. BNI is so much more than just a one-off job!

Next day delivery

26/7/09

At a recent seminar I attended, one of the points made by the speaker Rob Brown was that 'Speed Stuns' and I guess that in truth we all know that, but in practice things just slow us down.

Well, this week I was stunned by speed – twice!

I was visiting the Hogarth Chapter in Chiswick (London) and had offered to take a friend, who was substituting, along with me in my car as we both live in Teddington. After the meeting I was involved with the Leadership Team, so my friend went for a bit of window shopping. Unfortunately, when we arrived back at my office she discovered that she had left her diary in a bank she had popped into.

With the use of the internet and a couple of phone calls the diary was soon found. However, neither of us had time to return to Chiswick that day to recover it, and the bank couldn't post it, but my friend needed the diary urgently as it contained the details of all of her up-coming meetings. I suggested contacting a member of the Hogarth Chapter and seeing if they could help.

We chose a member who had an office near to the Chapter meeting place and gave them a call. The member in question said that it wouldn't be a problem to collect the diary and post it. It was better than nothing and in a day or so the diary would be returned.

Imagine my friend's delight when early the next morning the diary arrived on her desk! It just so happened that the same day I emailed the same Hogarth member for a couple of their company's catalogues and a few of their business cards. The next day they too arrived on my desk.

Delivering your sales literature fast is certainly impressive, but going to the trouble to collect something for someone you hardly know and getting it delivered the next day, is something special.

We talk a great deal about credibility in BNI, about knowing, liking, and trusting someone. Well, this new Hogarth member has certainly got off to a speedy start in my book.

I mentioned Rob Brown to the member concerned and that he had talked about how speed stunned, and their credibility rose even further, as their reply was *"only if you give the customer what they want"*. So, speed does stun and if you give your customer, or your fellow chapter member, what they want, your credibility will certainly rise.

The catalogue I asked for was a baby catalogue from Perfectly Happy People and you can contact Jane Johnstone by email at: jane@phpbaby.com

John Frye has fun!

28/7/09

BNI Tudor's photographer, John Frye, had some fun at his meeting this morning. He shot a couple of panoramas, each consisting of between six and eight shots, which he then 'stitched' together in Photoshop. As John says, it was a bit of fun for him, but I think the results are excellent, and it was a great way of showing the Chapter what he can do.

It's Summer!

13/8/09

The last few meetings that I have attended have each had three or four members absent, and when I have mentioned this to the Leadership Teams they have all pretty much said the same in reply, *"It's the holidays. What can we do?"* And, to a degree, I guess that I have to agree with them.

At one of the Chapters the Education Co-ordinator covered absence in their education slot. I myself have tried sending a link to my blog on substitutes to members that have not arrived for a meeting. But with some members it just seems that when the holiday season arrives, as they are not (for the next few weeks) looking for any business, they just don't bother thinking about their chapter.

If only these members understood the damage that they were doing to their credibility and their prospects of a good amount of future business.

Let's consider future business first. Most businesses benefit from a steady flow of work. Not feast followed by famine. And, every businessman must have heard that the time to advertise for more work is when you are busy, not when work has dried up.

So, when you return from your two or three week summer break, what you really need is a full order book, not several weeks of letting your customers (and fellow BNI members) know that you are open again for business. With reliable substitutes and a few well crafted 60 Seconds you can come back to a diary full of appointments.

But, even more important, is what holiday absence does to your credibility.

What does it say about you and your business if you can't find anyone to sub for you? Can't be bothered to find any substitutes? Your substitutes don't turn up? You don't give your substitutes a good and different 60 Seconds each week? Nothing good! Every one of the above will affect your credibility to a greater or lesser extent. So, if you want more business long-term from your Chapter, always find a substitute and never think that it doesn't matter if you don't find one. Because it does!

Crazy lazy scale

30/8/09

Anthony Wood, Membership Co-ordinator of the Harlequin Chapter in Kew, has put together a newsletter for his chapter. With the assistance of Annette Peppis, Joan D'Olier, Chris Stock, contributions from the other members of the group and a fast learning of Quark Express, Anthony produced a newsletter full of great tips, member profiles, examples of team work and the benefits of long-term membership of BNI.

He also introduced the concept of the Crazy Lazy Scale. A scale that measures the contributions made by members to their Chapter: at the bottom Lazy, (those members who just turn up to meetings) and at the other end, Crazy, (those members who live and breathe BNI).

Where do you think that you would come on Anthony's Crazy Lazy Scale?

Anthony also revealed the identity of the person that gave him the inspiration for the scale, his once fellow Chapter member and mentor. Why not read the Harlequin newsletter and see if you agree with him? (Page 3) The Networker http://www.bnitwickenham.co.uk/docs/thenetworker.pdf

Even Tiger Woods has a coach!

3/9/09

Imagine what it must be like to be the best in the world and yet be honest enough to admit that you can still get better...that you don't know it all...to

94

understand that often we can't see our own mistakes, and if we are not getting better at something, we are in fact getting worse...that we have to get better, at what we do, just to stand still.

Tiger Woods, has a near perfect golf swing, and yet he still has a coach to help him improve it.

So, as a BNI member how can we improve our performance as a member, and the amount of business we receive from our Chapter?

Well, like Tiger Woods we can be coached. And, rather than spend thousands of dollars as Tiger does, we can attend the BNI Workshops for free (well okay, we have to pay for a coffee and a sandwich). There is a BNI Workshop covering every part of what it takes to become a winning member and, what's more, a success outside of BNI.

And it's the benefits that these workshops provide outside of BNI which I believe is their real value. Doing everything better in your relationships with your fellow BNI members is one thing, but the way that you handle yourself with business contacts, and even personal relations, can be something far more valuable.

Just think about two of the BNI Workshops: Networking Skills and Presentation Skills. How much more successful do you think your business would be, if you were more confident when speaking to your clients, suppliers, your bank manager (when asking for a loan), or possible new contacts?

So, if you would like to give the very best you can, and gain the best from your fellow members in return, why not sign up for a Workshop today and gain from coaching just like Tiger Woods does?

It's all in the detail!

9/9/09

Some while ago I listened to a very clear and concise 10 Minutes presentation. The member concerned broke their presentation down into easy to understand sections: a little bit of history, what made them special, the three main areas of business that they provided, what kind of business they were looking for and how they could be introduced. The fact that made them different was their attention to detail, real attention to detail, they did things that other people didn't even think about, some things that you might not even notice. But afterwards, somehow, something made you think that it was special. It's just that you couldn't put your finger on what it was.

It was a great 10 Minutes and certainly had me believing in the company and their products.

As normal toward the end of the meeting, the Door Prize was awarded and this is where the credibility of the 10 Minutes Speaker, in my mind anyway, took a body-blow. The Door Prize was wrapped up in an old plastic bag! All that special attention to detail that had been talked about just evaporated and it was replaced by a doubt in my mind. Did they really pay that extra-special attention to detail?

So, to ensure the best possible referral opportunities, make sure that whatever you say you do and that whatever you say you can do is backed up in everything you do. Don't let just one preventable lack of detail ruin your brand and everything it stands for.

Write your own ten questions!

15/9/09

Have you ever had a One2One with a fellow member and afterwards wished that they had asked you different questions and that you had been able to tell them things about you and your business, but the opportunity to do so just never came up?

Well, how about writing your own Top Ten questions that you would like to be asked?

Only you know the most important things about your business: best clients, best way to introduce you, what makes you special, the great story that illustrates just how good you are, the type of business you are looking for.

96

So, why not make it easy for your fellow member and give them a head start? By providing ten questions to get your meeting off on the right footing you have far more chance of both parties getting the very most from your One2One.

Not only will coming up with ten questions benefit your One2Ones, but by doing so it will help you to think in more detail about your business and maybe help you focus on something that you had not thought about before.

I would suggest contacting the member concerned before your meeting to propose the idea, giving them the opportunity to come up with ten questions that they would like to be asked.

Don't forget, One2Ones are far more than a social, or even a great chance to get to know someone better, they are the best way of allowing a member to find you the perfect referral.

Please let me know how you get on.

Who shall I introduce the visitor to?

21/9/09

On the 1st October our Leadership Teams will change and over the past couple of weeks all the members taking new roles within our Chapters have been trained.

One of these groups being trained have been the Visitor Hosts and they now know what an important part they play in showing their Chapter at its best.

Part of this training is to whom they should introduce a visitor; first call the Chapter Director, but if they are busy then another of the Leadership Team. It is then left to that person to introduce the visitor to another member. Possibly another member of the Leadership Team or maybe a member of the visitor's Power Circle. Introducing a visitor to someone in their Power Circle – a related business – will not only help them to relax, as they will have things in common to talk about, but will also enable them to find out that BNI works for people in their own industry.

However, the most important people to introduce a visitor to are the members of the Membership Committee.

Why?

Well, if the visitor has liked what they have seen, hopefully they will put in an application to join the Chapter. The committee will then meet to consider the application and references will be taken up. And, pretty much, that will be that.

But, what about if, say half of the committee, have met the visitor and had a conversation with them? Discovered small things about them; what they like about their job, the sort of people they know, what their hobbies are, and maybe have an idea of what sort of person they are: their attitude, whether they mix well, are outgoing. Wouldn't that make deciding if they would make a good member of the group far easier?

So, if you are a Visitor Host and stuck for someone to introduce a visitor to, seek out a committee member and you will be helping your Chapter to accept better new members.

What a pit lane!

26/9/09

Thursday morning dawned bright and sunny over the Daytona Kart track at Sandown Park, Surrey. As the clock ticked past 9.00am the sound of the twin engines of the Pro-Karts could be heard firing up, ready for the Business Class Grand Prix.

Twenty-one drivers were going to compete over the 900 metre track for the honour of fastest chapter member. John James, last seen at Dancing Queen in Richmond, arranged the forty-minute competition as a great team-building exercise for the Chapter, but also as an opportunity to show that he could transfer his opportunist road driving skills to the race track.

The pre-race breakfast of bacon butties was supplied by Chapter member Sarah Burley (Hampton Hampers), as was the mouth-watering lunchtime spread and a photographic record of the event was captured by fellow Chapter member Daniela Justus (Babitonga Photography).

Qualifying soon sorted out the men from the boys – well the fast from the not so fast – and the grid was set for the race. When the flag dropped to start the race Mr. John James was left on the line. He says his kart wouldn't go. Personally, I think his eyes were firmly fixed on the pit lane. But more of that later!

The event was split into two twenty-minute races, with the results being combined to find the finishing positions. After a change of kart our soon to be Chapter Director, one John James, managed to secure second place in the first race, with the fastest Chapter lady being Katy Letman.

It was the second twenty-minute race that was more interesting. This was due to the starting grid better reflecting the true speeds and abilities of the drivers, and also because the confidence of the drivers and their circuit knowledge was better. However, over-confidence was taking hold, as were tired bodies! One notably confident driver was Lee Morris, who not only had a number of 'incidents' and spins, but also posted the fastest lap of the day.

The final result? In first place was Colin Kent (staff member at XGeneration), in second place John James (he proved his point!), with Lee Morris taking third. Our fastest lady was Katy Letman. It was a brilliant day, great for the Chapter, with networking continuing long after the chequered flag had dropped over lunch in the sunshine.

Oh. That Pit Lane. Unluckiest member of the day, me, I couldn't drive due to a recent operation, but it had its compensations!

I'm not buying from Amazon!

29/9/09

In fact I'm not buying from Tesco, Shell, Virgin, Interflora, Sony, Rymans, P&O, Dell, Cadbury, Disney, Ford, Barclays, my local newsagent, and certainly not Imperial Printers.

Why not? Because by doing so I will be helping these companies stay in business and, what's more, make a profit. Have I gone mad? No, I don't think so, but I'm pretty sure some BNI members have!

Visitor Days are a great way of growing a BNI Chapter and if run correctly can easily add anywhere between five and fifteen, or more, members to a group. These extra members make finding referrals far easier, but this is nothing compared to the extra business that is passed within the group. Every member will benefit from the extra referrals given, some of which will be worth thousands of pounds.

So, why do I think some members are mad?

Well, it's very simple. These members see nothing wrong in buying from Amazon and the rest, they gladly part with their cash, sometimes for little in return, all the time adding to these companies' profits. But, recently when it was suggested that a Chapter might have a Visitor Day, one of the objections against running the day was that some members did not want to grow their Chapter just so that BNI made money.

I have to say that words fail me!

Okay, so that's not strictly true – I've written a fair few. But that thinking is just so negative and short-sighted that I find it beyond belief.

I just can't believe that any member would not want more referrals, more business, maybe thousands of pounds worth of extra business, if not for them but their fellow members, just because BNI will make a few hundred pounds.

I might go as far as suggesting that these members are not really best suited to BNI and the philosophy of Givers Gain.

100

180 words!

5/10/09

Do you find it hard to finish your 60 Seconds in just a minute, and always end up having your punch-line cut?

Well, you are not alone as many members do. Some members try and get the all important message in by talking really fast as they sit down, others try and get extra time but are drowned out by a bell, or similar deterrent, while others just throw their hands in the air and give up. But all fail to make the best use of their 60 Seconds, and it is so easy with a little planning. And that really is the key – planning!

Hopefully you would never go to see a client without having your sales pitch ready, so why would you turn up at your Chapter meeting and think you can 'wing' it? Even the most gifted speakers can't really ad lib a 60 Seconds, unless they also have a stop-watch in their head. Maybe they can get close, but unless you are one of those lucky people, you have to plan and practise.

So, first write your 60 Seconds and hone it until your message is clear and concise. Then practise speaking it, not reading it, but saying it out loud. Most of us read faster than we speak, so it's really important to speak it out loud. And then learn it, so that you don't need your copy when you present your 60 Seconds.

With just a little planning you will never have to rush your 60 Seconds again, but, more importantly, you will never lose another punch-line! One last thing, 180 words is about the most you can say in a minute.

Do your bad members run your Chapter?

12/10/09

Over the past few months I've noticed that a number of Chapters have had trouble introducing a Chapter development idea, or some kind of accountability, into their groups and, in some cases, given up on the idea altogether. The reason for this has always been the same: a few members who don't want to take part, or think it's a bad idea, and make the most objections. And so as to not upset the group, because now these members have influenced other members, the idea is dropped and the Chapter doesn't put in place what it needs to in order to grow and gain more business for all.

Having studied this type of member, I have discovered that they are always the same – the ones that don't fully contribute. They don't give, take part, and would be shown for exactly that, if real accountability was introduced.

So, my message to you is Leadership Team, Membership Committee, or Chapter member, don't let bad members run your Chapter and stop you gaining all that is possible from your BNI Chapter.

A clear message!

26/10/09

We are always advised to keep our 60 Seconds and 10 Minutes presentations simple, to have a clear message, and not fill them full of jargon and buzz words. This advice is just as important with our Chapter education slots.

I saw a brilliant example of just how simple, clear, and yet powerful, an education slot can be at a recent visit to a chapter in the London North West area. (I have given the area as the figures used are actual figures from the PALMS data in the region.)

The education slot was given by Nikki Keeler the Chapter's estate agent after she had attended a recent Momentum workshop.

On a flip chart she wrote 'VISITORS', an arrow down to 'MEMBERS', another arrow to 'REFERRALS', and last an arrow down to 'BUSINESS'.

As members we all joined our chapters to get more business and the way that this works best is in large groups where everyone gives. We have all heard this before, but what made this education slot so powerful were the figures that she then gave. Real figures from local Chapters; Chapters that we knew!

A Chapter with 20, in the past year passed 454 Referrals, with £55,000 worth of business being thanked for. Another group, this time with 29 members, passed 1107 referrals, with business thanked for of £212,000. Next was a Chapter of 37 members, referrals 2022, and business done £598,000. And, finally a chapter of 46 members, passing 3108 referrals, with almost £1.6 million worth of business thanked for in the group.

The message was clear: if you wanted to grow your business, helping to grow your Chapter was a straightforward way of doing just that.

The average return per member in a Chapter of 20 was £2,750. By doubling the size of the group that average went up to over £34,000 per member.

As I say – the message is clear!

Phone a friend!

1/11/09

I don't know about you but I don't always find role-play easy. Role-play is not that hard in itself, but in a training room full of people, all pretending that they are meeting someone for the first time face-to-face, or sitting next to someone using your little finger and thumb as a phone, well it just doesn't feel real. And, let's face it – it's not!

But role-play and practice are actually very important if we are to be successful in finding both referrals and visitors for our Chapters. They are also just as important in our everyday business life, as a great telephone manner and confidence when meeting people for the first time will win us more business.

So, how do we practise more real and effective role-play?

Well, the answer is very simple – phone a friend. Not just on the spur of the moment, but arrange a time when it would be convenient. Maybe agree on a time between 10.00am and lunchtime one morning, or just after lunch one afternoon. It doesn't matter when, as long as your friend has time to take the call and is happy to play their part.

As a BNI member you already have scripts as to what to say, so that part is done for you. But I bet some of you are saying, 'I can't say that!' Well, guess what? You don't have to. What I would suggest is that you type the script as suggested into Word, then say it out loud. Any words that don't sound correct for you, or you stumble over, change to words that you would use. Once you are happy with the new script, you will have your version, a version that you are comfortable saying.

Then all you do is ring your friend, try it out, and ask for some feedback. Then try again another day, and so on, until you are happy with how you sound and your friend has not said that they are leaving the country.

At this point it is time to try it for real. I can promise you that you will be surprised at how good a result you get.

Just a couple of things to finish: enjoy yourself and if your friend is a fellow BNI member, return the favour.

Are you sitting comfortably?

21/11/09

Recently I was on a conference call, given by Area Director Phil Berg. Its subject was 'getting more visitors to your Chapter', and I have to say that as a Gold Badge member (pretty good at bringing visitors) of BNI, the content was just outstanding.

In fact, however good you are at bringing visitors to your chapter, you could not have hung up at the end of the call and not be better still.

Members often say that it is difficult to think of who to invite to their Chapters and Phil had at least twenty ideas on the subject; one of which was a visual interpretation of 'Follow your money'. And, it's so simple!

So, are you sitting comfortably?

It doesn't matter if you are reading this at home or in the office, it will work. It will even work in your garden, in fact just about anywhere.

All you have to do is look around you and start taking notes. Where did you get the carpet? The picture frames? Who made the bookshelves? Who decorated the room? Who put in the central heating? Where did you buy the curtains? Who decided on the colour scheme? Who made the cushions?

Get the idea?

And, what's great, each room of your house will give you a slightly different list, your garden another and your office yet another.

But, the best thing of all is that you know all of these people. Each one has supplied you, you know how good they are, and each would be more than happy to talk to you. After all, you are a customer of theirs.

So, make your list and start inviting all of those great suppliers you know.

The book you don't read won't help you!

29/11/09

I was asked recently why I was always reading a business book and my answer was very simple: development. After all, you can always learn. Plus, the more you know the easier things becomes.

One of the benefits I find is that by reading more than one book on any given subject, I learn more. The reason is that one author will explain a subject slightly differently to another and this difference, plus the repetition, help me to fix things in my head. Even then, I can always learn more about the subject.

This reminds me of a deal I made with a member some time ago when he couldn't see the point of going to Visitor Host training for a third time!

He was a Visitor Host at the time and just couldn't see the need of being trained yet again. So, I made him a deal. If he carried out the visitor host role perfectly at the next meeting he need not do the training. He knew that whatever he did, it could always be improved, so he attended the training without any more fuss.

While on the subject of repeat training, even if he could carry out the Visitor Host role perfectly, why would he not want to go to the Workshop and network with the other BNI members and gain possible new business?

So, every book you don't read won't help you, and it is the same with training; every workshop you don't attend can't help you or your business.

Two books that I can really recommend are 'The Jelly Effect' by Andy Bounds and 'Truth or Delusion' by Ivan Misner.

Can't get a sub!

21/12/09

I have to say that it always worries me when a member says this, especially if it's said by a long-term member. I know there are, on occasion, events that none of us can do anything about. But in reality these occasions are rare.

So, why do these words worry me?

Well, because not being able to get a sub can only really be for one of three reasons, and these are:
1. the member can't be bothered to find a sub,
2. the member has no contacts,
3. the member has contacts but none will sub for them.

And, each of these reasons is damaging to the member.

"Can't be bothered!" I'm sure I don't have to spell out what this does to a member's credibility. But the bottom line is fewer referrals.

Then there is *"Has no contacts"*. Again the member's credibility is put into question. Why are they in a networking group in the first place? But, far more important, without a good network of people they know, how is the member going to find referrals for their fellow members?

A member needs to Give in order to Gain (Givers Gain), so if they can't give, why are other members going to give to them? And, then we have

"have contacts but none will act as a sub". What does that signal to the other members of the Chapter? That the member has contacts but those contacts are not strong enough to be considered friends, or even people that like the member enough to do them a favour? BNI is based on know, like and trust. If a member's own contacts don't really like them, why should the Chapter members?

And, two last things on choosing a sub.

Please don't go for the easy option – the Super Sub, or BNI member you know will always sub. Why? Because, it is easy, no effort, and therefore what is that saying about you?

Lastly, *"my sub let me down; you can't surely mark me as absent!"* Well yes, your Membership Co-ordinator will. Do you know the reason that a member is most often let down by their sub? Answer: because, the member took the easy option.

As a member, you need to think carefully about who you ask to sub for you. It needs to be someone you have a great relationship with, someone who matters to you, and to whom you matter. Will your best friend let you down? I doubt it. Will some person you don't know, whose name you got from another member at the last moment? I'm not saying that they will, but there is a much greater chance.

So, next time you need a sub, think very carefully about the amount of effort you put into choosing them, as the right sub will enhance your credibility and, in turn, your referral rate.

YouTweet

23/12/09

Well by now the BNI YouTweet challenge is well underway and a variety of chapter videos have been posted on YouTube. Chapters have interpreted the challenge in a number of ways from the fairly straightforward chapter meeting, to songs, events, Christmas parties, the use of humour, and the just plain stylish!

The competition runs until the end of January 2010 and I for one can't wait to see the winning entries.

Some videos on You Tube

BNI - Business Class
http://www.youtube.com/watch?v=Pg5PZtIf6AY&fmt=22

BNI - Business Class
http://www.youtube.com/watch?v=sWuFaqB5VaY

BNI - Tudor
http://www.youtube.com/watch?v=pmHHqqL1z9k

BNI - Hogarth
http://www.youtube.com/watch?v=Be0S2JyCQaY

Merry Christmas!

A New Year

30/12/09

The next couple of weeks will see many New Year resolutions made and most broken! So, what will you do differently this year to change that pattern?

And no, don't make any is not the right answer!

I don't really like Smart Goals (S – significant, M – meaningful, A – achievable, R - realistic, T - timely), but most New Year resolutions are broken because they are unrealistic and to you, at any rate, are not meaningful.

In business, and therefore in BNI, as BNI is very much a part of our business, it is exactly the same. What business plans will you make for the New Year that will have gone astray by the beginning of February?

We all want to be more successful in 2010, and the best way to start is by reviewing this year and then making plans for next. Plans that mean something to us, we can see their value, and, most importantly, plans that are possible to achieve. So, what does this mean in terms of our BNI membership?

Well, for example, it doesn't mean planning to go to a Training Workshop every month, if you only managed to attend one workshop in the whole of this year. Sorry, but it's not going to happen – it's just not realistic.

What I believe would make the most difference is a small improvement in each of four areas: attendance (including subs), training, visitors and referrals. Have a think about how you have done in each of these areas this year. If you really have no idea, ask your Membership Co-ordinator for the information. Then aim to improve each just a little. When asked what do I think the minimum requirement of an average chapter member is, I say the following: no absences, an average of one referral per week, a visitor every two months, and attending a workshop twice in six months. Would this be a realistic plan for you, or are you already way ahead of this?

If you are great at bringing referrals, maybe you need to improve your visitor bringing – or, vice versa. You might be pretty good in three of the areas, so increase them a little, and poor in the fourth, so concentrate your efforts there.

The main thing is to review your past year and then plan improvements for next year that you see value in and want, and can, accomplish.

The bottom line is more business in 2010 and what you will do with the extra money!

Not on my letterhead!

16/1/10

I hear many reasons for not wanting to take part in Chapter launches, big visitor days and posting out invitation letters. Asking some members to send out forty letters is like asking them to run across burning coals naked, judging by the reaction you get. Then, after I am told that they could write a better letter, they add *"…and don't think I'm putting a BNI letter on my company's letterhead!"*

I really find this attitude very hard to understand. Why wouldn't any business want to have forty prospective customers see their company letterhead? – a letterhead that is well designed, tells the person what that company does, and is signed by someone looking for new business. I guess that is why we are all in BNI – new business.

Just this week I was having a One2One with a fairly new member of my Chapter, and we were talking about how important visitors are to a healthy Chapter, and how to invite them. He said that his aim was to post out five letters each week and, naturally, I asked him how things were going.

Pulling a sheet of paper out of the filing tray on his desk, he said far better than he had expected. He had a visitor for the next meeting – great! – but, even better, was that he had quoted on a job. The business that he had posted his letter to, on his company letterhead, read who the invitation was from and needed his service. And, the best part, he would never have mailed the company had it not been for his BNI inviting. Every invitation letter you send out, on your company letterhead, may not lead to a visitor for your Chapter, but it may just result in business for you. It certainly can't hurt you.

So, my message to you is this: if you don't like sending out invitation letters, BNI is all about marketing your business, so use BNI as an excuse and send out as many invitation letters as you can. You never know, you might even earn yourself a BNI Gold Badge!

A tough day at the office!

31/1/10

There are many reasons for attending our BNI Workshops, so it still astounds me when both new and long-term members tell me that they can't see the value to their business. Their company training is better, (I'm not even going to comment on that), they know all they need to know, they have been before, they don't have the time... The reasons for not attending seem almost endless!

And, this reminded me of an MST (Member Success Training) workshop I was at some months ago. One of my then Chapter Directors, David

McGeachie, of Tenant Finder, was there. He almost didn't come as he was tired and just fancied a beer. But, as he was new to the role of Chapter Director, he thought that he should make the effort and see what new members were being taught – something I think all Leadership Team members should do, not just the Chapter Director.

At all Workshops, the members present were asked to introduce themselves briefly. The members in the room ranged from those who had only been a member of their chapter for a matter of weeks, to one eight year member. One member, of just three weeks, was John Bishop, an estate agent.

During the coffee break David and John met and decided that they should meet at a later date for a coffee. John had a block of flats to rent, but they weren't in the area local to his office, they were in an area he didn't really know: Teddington. Yes, that is where David's business operates! Well, to cut a very successful story short. Tenant Finder won the contract to let the flats: a deal worth a fair amount of money. And, what's more, David and John are still working together.

So, if you only want one good reason for attending our workshops: it's networking. Because you never know, you might just meet your biggest customer there!

A boat in February!

4/2/10

The first week in February is International Networking Week and some time ago our Area Director, Dinah Liversidge, asked us, her Regional Directors, if we had any suggestions for an event.

A few days later I suggested a river boat trip on the Thames from Kingston, inviting a selection of members from each chapter in our region, some members from adjoining regions, other local networking groups, and some local business people.

The look on Dinah's face said you must be joking – a boat in winter! I just said, *"It's heated"*, and she replied, *"Let's go for it!"*

Tuesday the 2nd February saw around 90 people board the Turk Launches' New Southern Belle riverboat for a cruise from Kingston to Richmond and back. A wonderful buffet was served up by Hampton Hampers, live music by Helen Baden, with prizes supplied by BNI.

Amongst those on board were Dinah Liversidge, Richard Turk (Managing Director of Turk Launches), Tim Cook (National BNI Director), David O'Dell (Operations Director at BNI Head Office) and, of course, me.

Was it a good event? I think the following email I received this morning answers that.

Hi Dinah & David,

Many thanks for the invitation to the networking 'do' last evening. Rather nervous that it was an away day at over 100 miles round trip, but I am delighted I accepted.

It was a thoroughly enjoyable and entertaining evening. I made several very useful contacts, sorted out the purchase of a van for the business, together with the finance, and gave Tim some ideas re: the traffic lights! (It's not a league table unless you are top!) On top of that I gained another potentially excellent contact following my 60 Seconds!

Great idea to hold the meeting on a boat as nobody could leave early!

Once again many thanks. And kind regards
Alan Brooks, Clements Carpets – Bringing life to your home!
Mobile 07947 534126, Shop 01923 256006

That's my job!

28/2/10

This is a phrase I hear a great deal from BNI category hogs. And sadly, it is usually from members of smaller Chapters, who are vulnerable about their own ability in business, but who also don't see the benefits of a great network. There are many examples: the IFA who thinks that they can cover mortgages and insurance as well, the web designer who also wants SEO and

Google business, the printer who of course does design (don't we all), and the builder that covers every trade – including some that you have never heard of. What these members don't see is the damage that they are doing to their own business, their credibility and that of the Chapter as a whole.

A good Power Team will give its members over 60% of the referrals that an individual member will receive from their Chapter. For this to be really effective the Power Team needs to have at least six members: members that are in a related category. Again, there are many examples, but I will pick just one, the Financial. In this Power Team the most usual categories are: Accountant, Banker, Insurance Broker, IFA, Solicitor, Mortgage Broker and Book Keeper.

Each of these members will have their own contacts; a good networker will have as many as one thousand (it doesn't really matter what the number is, it's the principle that matters). So, as a whole this group has seven thousand contacts. Now imagine what happens if the IFA category hogs and an insurance and mortgage broker don't join the group. Suddenly the group only has five members and five thousand contacts. Imagine then what happens if the accountant category hogs and a book keeper doesn't join.

In large, successful Chapters there are often two solicitors, two insurance brokers, and another financial person. Ten members with ten thousand contacts. Whereas in the 'category hogs' Chapter just four members with four thousand contacts. Which do you think does the most business?

So, my message to you? If you are a builder, don't get up and in your 60 Seconds say you cover every trade going, but instead get every trade you can into your Chapter. Networking is about having a great network of people you, know, like, and trust. It is not about having sole access to your Chapter and the members that, at most, will give you 30% of your referrals.

Are you brave enough to be accountable?

21/3/10

Every week at our BNI meetings the Membership Co-ordinator says when describing his role in the Chapter, "…*Like any good business, we set goals and monitor our progress towards achieving those goals."* But, those are Chapter goals. How many of us set personal goals and monitor those?

I believe that if every Chapter member sets personal goals, even average ones, every Chapter would be successful. Their Chapter would be in the 'Green' and every member would be getting a good return on their investment. So, what's average?

Well, in my mind average is: an average of one referral per week, a visitor once every two months, and attending a workshop once every three months. Do the maths yourself and see what the results would be for your Chapter if every member did this. Even for an average-sized Chapter it would mean three visitors every week!

Think what would happen if, as a member, you were better than average, because if you are anything like me I don't like being just average. But, the question is, are you brave enough to be accountable?

Every month the Secretary/Treasurer should print off the Chapter Roster sheet, which includes a 'league table' of the Chapter members' performance for the month, and leave it on the sign-in table so that members can see who is doing what. However, in many Chapters this is not done, for fear of upsetting some members.

So, if you are brave enough to be accountable, ask your Secretary/Treasurer for the sheet, check your performance and then watch your Chapter improve and make more money!

Sorry – no referrals this week!

2/4/10

We've all heard it: a member gets up and says they have no referrals this week and then usually adds some poor excuse. What they really mean is that they have done nothing for their fellow members that week.

However, I'm not going to go into that. What gets me is that I have never heard anyone get up and say, *"Sorry – no visitors this week"*. And, I have to say, that I have thought long and hard about this and this is my conclusion. The reason has to be for one of the following: 1) we do not place enough value on visitors, or 2) most members want to receive referrals and so in their own mind it is only referrals that matter.

Now, I'm not suggesting that we should start saying we are sorry for not having a visitor, as our Chapters shouldn't allow us to say sorry for not having a referral, but I do think we need to change the mindset of members thinking that it is only referrals that count. Maybe this is why some Chapters find it hard to grow – because they don't see the true value of visitors.

So, how can we change this way of thinking?

Well, I have two ideas to start with. Firstly, the Chapter can give more recognition to those members who bring visitors each week. Most Chapters clap if a member has three of more referrals in a week. How about a round of applause if a member brings two visitors or more?

Most Chapter Directors give the Referral Notable Networker award first. How about instead presenting the Visitor Notable Networker award first?

Then, as members, instead of thinking *"I must have a referral this week"*, how about thinking *"I must find a visitor this week"* instead? As the more visitors our Chapter has, the more members it will have, which in turn will lead to more referrals and lastly to more business for the group.

What's amazing about this approach of *"I must find a visitor"* is that it would also go a long way to solving the *"Sorry – no referrals this week"* problem!

What do you think?

Power Teams – the best way to build your Chapter?

10/4/10

Well, I would have to say yes. And, I will explain why. But first, I want to make it clear what a Power Team is and for this it is best to take the definition directly from the BNI website.

A Power Team is a group of related professions that work with the same clients but do not take business away from each other. So, with what a Power Team is now clear, why do I think growing a Chapter by inviting people from your Power Team is the best way of growing a Chapter?

Almost without the need for any other reason is the fact that 60% of a member's referrals will come from other members of their Power Team. I believe that this alone is reason enough for every member to want to be part of the largest Power Team possible.

But, for those that want another reason, and although more relevant to Chapters in the low thirties and smaller, it is this. When we think about adding twelve members to our Chapters, so that we can gain the best from it, the task seems pretty daunting. But if we just think about adding two members to our Power Team it suddenly seems, and is, in fact, far easier.

And, the great thing about that? There are six Power Teams in each BNI Chapter: Property, Financial, Wedding Services, Trades, Business Services and Health & Wellness. Add two members each to those and guess what? You have your twelve new members!

So, what are you waiting for? Speak to the other members of your current Power Team, decide what two categories you need, get inviting and just watch your Chapter grow!

Could you be Columbo?

22/4/10

I'm sure you know who I mean. The crumpled TV cop of the 70s who always got his man (or woman).

No. I'm not suggesting that you buy a battered old car and a dog, but his famous *"Just one more thing"* question, always said as if an afterthought, really works well for me.

BNI and word-of-mouth is all about not having to cold-call. After all, don't we recommend each other? But sometimes it's fun to get out of your comfort zone and if you do, and you are brave enough, you can get some amazing results.

So, obviously this is about face-to-face contact, but I don't in truth consider it cold-calling, as it's not trying to sell anything. I'm just popping in to a local company for a chat, to tell them about the group of amazing business people I work with and maybe they would like to meet them. That's it!

They either say yes or no. Sometimes I get a maybe. But whether it is no or maybe I get to leave an invite to my Chapter. If yes, I invite them to the next meeting. And, then I leave.

But, just as I am about to reach the door comes the Columbo moment!

I turn and say, *"Oh. I'm a printer by the way. Is it okay if I leave you my card? Just in case."* I've never had anyone say no, but I have had more than one person ask me to quote on some work.

Having a chat with someone is nothing like cold-calling and you never know you might just get a visitor, client, or, if you are very lucky, both.

Please let me know how you get on.

I'm not referring to them!

26/4/10

Do you have a person in your Chapter that you don't refer to? If you do – have you ever told them why?

Now there may be many reasons for not referring to someone: you already have a long-term supplier that you refer to in that category, you really just don't mix with the right sort of people, your best friend is in the same line of business, and even that you just don't like the person.

What about if it is because you think the person is unreliable, they don't seem professional, there is a negative opinion of them in the group or they have never tried to get to know you? Don't you owe it to them to tell them?

If you don't tell them, they are losing out on business from the group, may never become a good member and in the end leave because they don't think BNI works. Now, of course there is a risk in telling them. I guess that might be why we avoid doing it, and they might not take any notice. But, what if they did listen?

Not only listen and change, but thank you and become a good member of the group. And, guess who would then be at the top of their referral to look for list! You might even make a long term change to their whole business.

So, is there someone in you Chapter that you don't refer to? How about arranging a One2One with them and letting them know?

Note: I must give credit for this blog to Ewan Sturman and his Workshop at the recent BNI European Conference.

I'm too busy!

3/5/10

I've heard this comment a fair few times recently when members have been talking about their lack of contribution to their groups. Too busy!?

How can you be too busy to do your job? But then I guess that's the crunch: far too many BNI members think that working for their Chapter members is an extra to their job – something they do if they get time!

What these members don't understand is that their chapter (collectively) could become their biggest client, but only if it is treated as such.

So what do I mean? Well, would you let your largest client down? Any client for that matter? Not bother to let them know that you weren't going to turn up for a meeting? Or tell them that you were busy to see them and had more important things to do? Somehow I don't think so and, if you did, I don't think that they would stay your biggest client for long.

Not having a contribution for your meeting (because you've been too busy working) means you have not had time for any member of the group and yet you are hoping for a referral from them. You are hoping that someone in the room has put in some effort to find you something and has not been busy doing their job.

What if, on the other hand, they are just as busy as you are but they see BNI as part of their job, part of what they have committed to, that they really value the members of their group? Just like great clients.

And, an even simpler point, do you really think that anyone will be looking to help you if you have no time to help them?

Your BNI Chapter is in every way just as important as any other part of your business. You just have to think it is – then it will be. And, I promise you will be surprised at the results when you do!

Is your Notable Networker certificate notable?

15/5/10

In our Chapters every month we recognise two outstanding members by presenting them with notable networker certificates and, on occasion, a blue badge. But, quite often, the quality of the certificate presented does not reflect the true achievement of the member.

I've seen a certificate written in biro just passed down the table. What value does that put on the presentation and what the member has done? How do you think that member feels?

So, first off, the certificate should be in a nice frame but, more importantly, it must be beautifully written. Now, few of us have lovely hand-writing, let alone are skilled in calligraphy. So, how about this for an idea that I was given by Colin Read, Area Director, from Scotland South and East?

For a beautiful looking certificate set up a template in Word or Publisher, using a font such as Lucida Calligraphy (bold), and then every certificate your Chapter presents will match the achievements of your members.

So simple, but I've never thought of doing it!

Are you good enough to be part of the next Leadership Team?

23/5/10

I know we are only seven weeks into the current term but choosing our next teams will be upon us before we know it and a comment I heard, just the other day, by a member got me thinking!

What they said was how pleased they were not to be asked to take a place on the current team.

Not just the Leadership Team but any position at all!

Now I don't know about you, but if I wasn't considered for a place on the team I would be, well, pretty upset, that both the outgoing and incoming teams didn't think me good enough to help the chapter in going forward. What would that say about me as a member?

So, rather than thinking you 'got off' by not being asked to be on the team, instead wonder why you weren't considered good enough to be part of it.

What is stopping you from being looked at as a great member?

Do you contribute enough? Go to training? Help in the group? Arrive on time? Are you a positive member? Look the part? Do you really 'get' BNI?

So, being asked to be on the Leadership Team means that you are thought of as a great member of your Chapter. Someone that can be trusted and relied upon, someone who is more likely to be thought of by fellow members, and BNI Directors, when they are out talking to their contacts, which in turn will lead to more opportunities.

In seven weeks time the next Leadership Teams will start to be planned, which means that every one of us has plenty of time to make sure that we are good enough to be considered for that next team.

And, guess what? If we are all great members, imagine what that will do to our Chapters and the amount of business that every one of us will receive!

High speed 21st Century IFA

6/6/10

Some members find it very difficult to prepare for their 10 Minutes. In fact, I know some members that avoid their 10 Minutes as if it were the plague. But it does not have to be like this.

The most obvious answer to the problem is to attend the Presentation Skills Workshop. However, that will only solve part of the problem. Even armed with tips on how to stand, speak, where to look, layout of your presentation and much more, there is still the problem of the exact content and, more importantly, will your fellow members actually be interested enough in what you are saying not to fall asleep!

Then of course there is still the problem of confidence. For some members 60 Seconds is just about all they can manage and 10 Minutes? Well, that is a whole different world.

So, what can we do about this? Two things. Firstly, make your presentation about something you enjoy and secondly, combine that with business. The confidence will come as you are relaxed, chatting about something you really understand and love.

Now, I'm not suggesting that you don't enjoy or understand your job; it's just that some jobs are more difficult to talk about than others! Carpet cleaning for example. But how about if you actually clean a carpet during your 10 Minutes?

A brilliant example of this type of thing happened in my chapter (Business Class) just recently. Now, Richard Bailey doesn't lack confidence, but he is an IFA and wears a grey suit, and there are those around that think financial advice and those that give it are well, shall we just say, a little boring!

Not so Richard. After all, he races motorbikes all around Europe, and has the worn-out knee pads to prove just how fast he goes and how close to the ground he gets. His 10 Minutes was a mix of personal pictures and graphs showing the performance of his clients' portfolios. Each photograph having a bearing on the next was very clever, interesting, and got his message across in a fun way that we all could grasp. Something that he told us was that in order to get the perfect lap on his motorbike, i.e. the fastest time, it was all about hitting the exact spot on each corner, every lap. Total concentration and consistency were required – and that it was just the same when managing a client's portfolio.

So, if you have a 10 Minutes coming up, please take advantage of it. It's one of the best ways of helping your fellow members find you referrals. Just make it fun: include something that you find it easy to talk about or to demonstrate, and you will find that not only will you get your message across, but that it will be easy, and you wished you had more time.

Does your meeting have three visitors each week?

20/6/10

There are many ways in which you can tell if your chapter is healthy or not, but the number of visitors your Chapter has each week is an easy way of telling if your Chapter is growing or in decline.

Over the long term three or more visitors each week mean the Chapter is growing, whereas two or fewer visitors mean that the chapter is in decline.

Now you may be wondering why this should be the case and the answer is simple. On average all Chapters lose one member per month. Now before you say *"Not my Chapter!"* remember I said on average. Some Chapters don't lose that number, but then others lose more. In fact, my own Chapter has lost four members in the past month – it really does happen!

So, during the term of a Leadership team, your chapter could lose up to six members (maybe more). Therefore, just to remain a group of the same size, you need six new members. Now, again on average, one out of every five eligible visitors will join your Chapter. However, we all get a lot of 'other' visitors as well, so the joining rate is actually more like one in every eight visitors.

This is where the maths comes in!

For your Chapter to remain the same size you therefore need six new members, which means that with one in eight visitors joining you need 48 visitors in the six months of your Leadership Team. If we divide 48 by 26 (6 months) the result is 1.85 visitors per week. (Let's call it two so there's no blood).

And, it doesn't matter what size your Chapter is, the facts are the same. Under two visitors a week and your Chapter size is in decline and this means less business for all.

But, here's the best bit. On average, if you are in a Chapter of 26 members, each member only has to bring one visitor every two months! How easy is that?

Why not work out the number of visitors a member needs to bring in a Leadership Team term for your own Chapter and set that as a member target?

Nothing to contribute!

24/6/10

Every BNI member knows that there are three ways in which you can contribute at your meetings each week:

A visitor (my favourite, as visitors bring so much to our meetings and if they become members add even more), A referral, A testimonial.

Now, as I have said before, I think visitors are undervalued by many members because they don't see any immediate gain for themselves, unlike with a referral, but I also think the same is true of the testimonial. And, this is because some members see the testimonial as a 'cop out'; a member has nothing else, so let's write a testimonial.

But again, these members are missing the point. A brilliant testimonial can be great for the Chapter in a number of ways: it lifts the group (as it is positive), shows visitors how professional the members of the Chapter are, raises the credibility of the member being given the testimonial, and in turn increases the number of referrals for that member and the Chapter as a whole. And, talking of being positive...

Many great meetings are destroyed when a member stands up and says 'Nothing this week'. And if a second or third member follows suit, with a nothing, you can see all the energy drain from the other members.

So, please, if nothing else give a verbal testimonial. If not for a member, then how about for a Workshop, Members' Day, help from your RD/AD, or BNI in general? It's not perfect, but so much better than – 'nothing'!

I would just like to add two things here. I think all Chapter Directors should allow all members to be positive in their meetings and members please don't use the verbal testimonial as a 'cop out'.

Oh, one last thing. Membership Co-ordinators, what do you do if a member seems to be taking 'advantage' of the verbal testimonial? Answer: discuss the member at your next committee meeting and take the appropriate action.

Will your networking work?

26/6/10

Will your networking work? Well, the easy answer is yes. But, here's the rub: only if you are putting in enough effort. It doesn't matter how good you may be, how good your business is, or how good a networker you are – if you are not spending enough time networking it won't work!

At the London BNI Members' Day yesterday Dr. Ivan Miser, founder of BNI, told us that in some research that he has conducted successful networkers, those that really benefit from their networking, spend over six hours a week in productive networking. However, those that said networking didn't work for them spent less than two hours a week networking.

So, are you expecting outstanding results from your networking without putting in the necessary hours?

To find out, why not record all of your effective networking hours over the next month and see how many hours per week, on average, you are networking for?

More than six hours and the odds are that your networking is working for you, less than that, well I think you already know the answer!

As a guide you need to be networking for at least four hours a week in addition to your Chapter meeting.

Memory hook?

7/7/10

Most successful companies have a memory hook, although we may think of them more as their slogans: Nike – Just Do It; KFC – Finger Lickin' Good; Tesco – Every Little Helps.

Then, of course, there are our fellow BNI members and here we have some great examples of memory hooks (straplines): Simply Spreadsheets – *We take the Hell out of Excel!*; Imperial Printers – *We will print you any colour you like, but it will always be green*; and IFA Richard Bailey – *Don't be a thicky, refer them to Dicky.*

At a recent BNI workshop, Tom Fleming, BNI Executive Director of West Central Florida, suggested that BNI Chapters should also have a memory hook, one that the Chapter Director (President) could use each week, during the meeting and as an email signature, etc. And I have to say, I think it is a brilliant idea.

Every week the members and visitors alike would hear the goal of the group, its belief, the Chapter's message. What a great way to let everyone know the future vision of the Chapter. I've even come up with a few ideas: Green and Going for Forty; Turning contacts into contracts (Niri Patel); BNI Business Class – we make our members more money (just an idea team!). So, what do you think? Would a memory hook for your Chapter help your vision? Maybe, it would even give your Chapter a vision, a goal. And, who would choose your Chapter's memory hook?

It would be great to hear your views and, in time, any result should you decide to use one.

You don't have to be terrific but it helps to be specific!

14/7/10

I heard this memory hook recently at a BNI directors' meeting and I have to say that, not only is it clever, but it is also true. In fact, just this last week the point was really hammered home to me.

The web designer in my group, who himself has a great memory hook, *"This is my business card, it may not build you a website, but it will start a conversation"*, always presents a clear and concise 60 Seconds. He more often than not asks for a company that he would like to be introduced to. I have had a One2One with him, and seen his 10 Minutes. So, I pretty much know what he does. I like him and he is very credible; his company has built some fantastic websites.

And yet I still missed a referral opportunity for him! Last week he asked for a company by name. I knew them, they are a contact of mine, so I phoned my friend and asked if they would take his call. They said they would have loved to but unfortunately they had their website redesigned just six months ago. I was gutted!

Now being specific didn't work out this time, the luck of timing, but by being specific I was given something I could follow up on easily and so did. I had never before given this contact any thought and I hate to think of the number of referral opportunities that pass us by because we aren't given something positive to look for.

So, be as specific as you can when asking for referrals. It will, (timing aside), make a big difference to the number and quality of the referrals you receive.

Have you seen your Chapter members' websites?

25/7/10

I was having a One2One recently with Hannah Liversidge of Reliable Roofer; she was showing me the basics of Wordpress, so that I could make a start on a new blog that I am writing.

We discussed the best ways in which we could help each other and the kind of business that we were both looking for. However, most of the time was spent on producing my first blog. 'David's Better Business Blog' is my Blog's title and 'Have a Networking Goal' my first Blog.

Obviously this lead to us talking about social media as a whole: Twitter, LinkedIn, Facebook, Ecademy, different blogging software, HootSuite, and of course Google. By this time we had moved on to our own websites and the importance of keeping them fresh and updated. Hannah asked if I had seen their website recently, as it had been updated, and I had to admit that I hadn't.

This got me to thinking about the websites of the members in my own Chapter and how many I had looked at recently. It then made me realise that there were some of their websites that I had never even seen.

Something of a shock! So, I guess, is that just me? Or, are all we all guilty of not taking the time to look at each others' sites?

We could learn so much, especially about new members. And, how about checking out the website of someone we are going to have a One2One with before we go?

It's certainly something that I am going to do and I can't help but think that it will not only improve my One2Ones, but will also increase the number of referrals that I give. What do you think?

I don't know anybody!

31/7/10

A phrase I often hear from members when asked about inviting visitors or finding referrals is *"I don't know anyone"* or *"I never see anyone; I work on my own."*

I have to say this not only worries me but that also, more importantly, I don't believe it. It worries me because all of us completed an application form to join our Chapters and question 7 on the application form asks: What is your ability to bring qualified referrals and/or visitors to the Chapter? Every one of us has entered an answer: member of golf club, chamber, Rotary, PTA, or maybe a large customer base, many years in business and much more. And, if we didn't, why were we accepted by the Chapter's membership committee?

So, really we must all know lots of people. Therefore, this brings me to the conclusion that members do in fact know a great many people (I don't believe that they don't), it's just that they don't realise it!

So, how about running a little test? It will take you no more than 15 minutes. Make a list of all the groups that you are connected with, for example, mobile phone contacts, email address book, family, friends, business contacts, suppliers, customers, chamber, church, sports clubs, choir, PTA, band, pub, LinkedIn, Facebook, university, boat club – list them all. Then list the first five people from each group that just pop into your mind; I bet it will be more like 10 names in every case!

Finally, add up how many names you have. I really would be surprised if it were less than one hundred.

Now, in front of you, is a database personal only to you: a list of people, not only to invite to your Chapter but who are also a rich source of referrals.

These people are your best contacts – please never say that you don't know anyone ever again. But, better still, make a difference at your Chapter.

Could you be a great actor?

25/8/10

In our Chapters we don't have competition as far as our individual categories are concerned. If there is a printer there can't be another in your Chapter, likewise for a business mentor, and so on.

But, how about the competition to have our 60 Seconds remembered?

If your Chapter has over thirty members, each week there are thirty plus 60 Seconds to listen to and remember. But, let's be honest, that's not going to happen! How many 60 Seconds do you remember each week? Six or seven maybe? So, this means that as a member we need to have a really memorable 60 Seconds if our message is to be remembered, and we are to be in the forefront of our fellow members' minds. Because that is the only way to consistently get referrals from our Chapter. We need to be remembered. In fact, better still, we need to be a story worth telling.

So, how about this for an idea? Act your 60 Seconds! Choose someone famous and then do your 60 Seconds in their style. I guarantee you will be remembered! Imagine, for example, your 60 Seconds being presented by Churchill, or David Frost, or Ann Robinson.

And, what's more, it will be great fun. Let me know how you get on.

It's a trade dispute!

31/8/10

We are often told that bad workmanship and money-owing are trade disputes and nothing to do with our Chapter, but I don't agree with this for two reasons. Both my reasons are to do with money owed, but equally apply to bad work. What I must make clear, however, is that one, you are not in the wrong, and two, that everything has been done to sort the problem out. Then I really do believe that it is a Chapter matter.

The first case was to do with a member who owed money to another member but was just not paying. He promised to, but never quite got around to it; there was always an apparently good reason. I then discovered the same member owed money to another member, with the same pattern of non-payment. Trade disputes: nothing to do with the Chapters concerned. However, he ended up leaving a trail of unpaid accounts behind him, something that may not have happened if a Chapter's committee had got involved and were allowed to act.

The second case was in fact two cases, where money was owed and then when asked for the people who owed started to complain about bad workmanship, the supplier being un-professional. They made stuff up and put it in writing (just in case it went to court) and ended by sending abusive emails. This has clearly passed the trade dispute stage and in my opinion is now a Code of Ethics issue.

But, the members concerned didn't want to cause a fuss or be seen to be causing trouble. Well, to my mind, that's what these non-paying members count on: nothing being said and keeping their positions in their Chapters with no one else knowing what they are really like. Well, my advice is let the Membership Co-ordinator know and allow the Chapter's committee to deal with the matter. If the person concerned is worried about their credibility you may get your money, or they may just leave, but at least you will have stopped anyone else getting hurt.

However, please remember what I said at the beginning, you must be honest about your side of the deal and your complaint must be in writing. Don't expect your committee to act if you won't put the details down on paper.

I mentioned the BNI Code of Ethics, of which, number two says, I will be truthful with members and their referrals, and number 6 says, I will display a positive and supportive attitude with BNI members. Is that what these non-paying members are doing? Trust is a big part of BNI, of our Chapters, and what we owe each other as members.

Note: As always this is only my view and not necessarily the view of BNI.

Have you just applied to join BNI?

21/9/10

Firstly, I would just like to say that you made a great decision. I've been a member for seven years now and I have to say that it was one of the best moves I ever made. And secondly, if you really get involved and treat your chapter as part of your business, not only will you get a considerable return on your investment, but you will have a lot of fun.

However, the real purpose of this Blog, is to get you off to a flying start. But, you will have to act fast!

How would you like to take a couple of visitors to your next meeting?

If your answer is yes, it's easy. But, what's more important, is that your new colleagues will be pretty impressed and you will have started to build your credibility and those good relationships.

So, how do you find a couple of visitors for next week? It's simple!

At your next Chapter meeting you should be inducted into your group: it's really important but also a bit of fun. So, why not take along a couple of friends to share in your moment? Okay, they might not want to join, but they might need the services of some of the members, and knowing more about what you do they may even find you some referrals in the future.

What do you think? Let me know how you get on.

All your Chapter members in a little box!

2/10/10

In my Chapter, over the past six months, 29% of the business we have received has come from our visitors – people who have never joined. Which, when you think about it, is reason enough to want visitors every week at your meeting.

However, I'm sure that this is just a very small amount compared to what it could be. After all, how many of us keep in contact with a visitor who comes once never to be seen again at our Chapter. Further, have we any idea how many of our business cards a visitor takes when the Chapter business card box is passed round? I can guarantee you it is not many.

So, it is interesting that recently I have noticed a number of the Chapters I visit have made up little packs of cards with a complete set of the Chapter members' business cards in. Sometimes they are just wrapped by a rubber band, sometimes in a small envelope, sometimes even in an A4 wallet with other leaflets, etc.

But, one of the best I have seen is all the cards put in a little business card box with a message that says 'Thank you for visiting our Chapter today. This box contains all of the business cards of our members, you may not need our services at the moment, but if you do in the future please don't hesitate to give any one of us a call.' What a great idea!

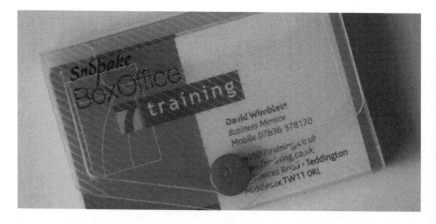

The boxes are from Snopake and are called BoxOffice – Business Card Size. It took me a while to find a supplier but if you are interested they are – Xpress Solutions.

So, how about a little experiment?

See what percentage of your Chapter's business came from visitors in the past six months and then for the next six months give all of your visitors a set of the Chapter's business cards and see what the difference is.

Hogarth's got talent!

13/10/10

There are members that can't see the benefit of socials: what's it going to do for my business?

I've often heard things like, *"I don't do socials"*, *"I haven't the time for that sort of thing"*, even, *"I don't need any more friends"*.

The thing that gets me is that we talk a great deal about, know, like and trust in BNI. LIKE!

I'm sure that I am not alone here but I enjoy doing business with people I like. We buy people, not products. So, how can socials not be important? They are the best way to get to know people, can often lead to a major mind shift about a person, and in turn to lots more business.

And, nothing was more the case than the recent Hogarth's Got Talent evening, where, along with my fellow judges, Piers Morgan (Tony Winyard), and Amanda Holden (Gary Morgan), yes, I was Simon Cowell, I got to see a great many of the Hogarth members in a totally different light.

Amanda Holden
Simon C

First up were Sebastian Wozniak and Jakub Kosiec, both giants of men, who performed a tug-of-war with a piece of string! They brought the house down and the benchmark for the evening was set. What's more, the Chapter would never view these two men in quite the same light again!

What followed was an amazing array of talent. Well, some of it was (Simon Cowell speaking here).

We were entertained with dance, standup (Colin Woodley), song, music, a BNI poem in the style of Pam Ayres, Phil and Ben the flower pot men with, of course, little weed (Phil Tait, Ben Walsh and Jane Johnstone) and, two men, two new members, who murdered one of my all time favourite songs 'I've got you Dave!' I mean 'I've got you Babe' by Sonny and Cher (Robin Curtis and Dave Saunders).

It was an incredible evening for everyone, even us judges, as everyone was a winner. And, I am sure that even more business will now be passed at Hogarth because of the improved friendship of the members.

It was an amazing evening in Chiswick!

If your Chapter is not big on socials, why not try one, and see if your business increases because of it?

Your Secretary/Treasurer is speaking!

17/10/10

One of the most important parts of our BNI meetings is the Secretary/Treasurer's Visitor Statement. We all know it, *"For the visitors here today, we welcome..."*, but it is so often one of the most poorly executed parts of the meeting.

Why? To be honest I'm not sure.

I've heard, *"It's a hard sell"*, *"We sound desperate"*, I feel uncomfortable saying it', *"It sounds a lot of money"*, *"I feel guilty asking for money"*, and much more.

But, as I say, I just don't get it! We are all members, so didn't we all hear exactly the same thing? We can't have thought any of those things, so why would anyone else?

However, this does lead me to two points, 1) if a Secretary/Treasurer can't read the statement with confidence, maybe they are the wrong person for the job and 2) if they do read it, sounding desperate, like it's a hard sell, making it sound like membership is not good value, that they could be affecting the conversion of your visitors into members.

Further, and I have to thank Ashley Winston (Palmdale Motors) for this, what are you, as a member, doing when the statement is being read? Again, unless you are paying attention to the Secretary/Treasurer, actually listening to them, looking at them, you could be adversely affecting the number of visitors that apply to join your Chapter.

Little things done well can make a really big difference to the result of any action, so why take a chance with such an important part of our meeting?

Absent again!

25/10/10

What should you do if your Chapter has five members missing one week and then seven the next?

The answer is easy! The Membership Co-ordinator and committee must follow the BNI policies, no matter who the members concerned are. There is no such thing as, *"But they're a good member"*. Why? Because a good member would not put the committee in a position where they had to take action that they thought was tough.

Successful Chapters are the result of strong committees, not nasty committees, but committees that follow the policies for the benefit of all the members, not just a few who think the rules don't apply to them. It's so much more than just about the policies. Chapters lose good members when things are allowed to slip because why should they make the effort, if other members don't have to.

Then, of course, there are the practical things. As a member, how would you feel about these absent members missing your 10 Minutes or your 60 Seconds? How are they going to find you good referrals? If they can't be bothered to turn up for the meeting (find a substitute), can you really refer them? Might they let down your best contacts?

Following the policies may lose you a few members, but it will ensure that you keep the good ones, and in the long run build a far stronger and successful Chapter!

They are in your phone!

3/11/10

Where to find potential visitors is a constant problem for many BNI members. Some take the easy option and head straight for an online directory, while others go to incredible lengths to find a visitor. Often spending hours without success. It's no wonder they give up and stop looking.

But, these members are missing an easy trick: people they already know!

BNI is a word-of-mouth organisation, but as soon as visitors are mentioned members seem to forget the people they know and instead start cold-calling.

It never ceases to amaze me.

Anyway, back to the easy trick. Just look at the address book on your mobile phone – these are your closest contacts. Have you invited them all? If not, then there are your next visitors. If yes, well the next question is, have you asked them for a recommendation? Do they know a good, whoever it is that you are looking for, to invite?

These people are your 'Trusted Third Party' contacts: they come recommended and so do you.

So, if you are finding who to invite difficult, just get out your mobile phone and start making those calls. Please let me know how you get on.

29% isn't just the title of a great book!

5/11/10

At the end of the day, we are all in BNI for more business and we all know that large Chapters produce more referrals and, in turn, more business. However, it's not that easy, is it?!

For some reason, many members see growing their chapters as something you have to do for the good of BNI. We have to bring lots of visitors – every week! Now, large Chapters are good for BNI, that's how BNI make their money, but they're even better for us as members. You just need to do the maths. Forty members times the membership fee, against one fortieth of the business passed in a forty strong Chapter. There is just no comparison!

Plus, how about this fact to make the inviting of visitors even more worth-while – every single week!

Most visitors don't join our Chapters. At best it is one out of every four visitors. But, in the last six months, in my Chapter, visitors were thanked for 29% of the business passed! That is business from people who aren't members of BNI. Now, if that's not a good reason to have visitors at your meeting every week, I really don't know what is!

Forget the fact that the meetings are better, we have more fun, there's more energy in the room, that they may become members, great friends even. Just think about that 29%.

Do you know how much visitors bring to your Chapter?

Who runs your Chapter?

13/11/10

I was asked recently who actually ran a BNI Chapter and the easy answer is the Leadership Team. But, like most things, it depends on who's asking and why!

So, I will expand a little and use a company set-up as my analogy.

Obviously the Leadership Team runs the Chapter, but with the help of the Membership Committee (HR, marketing, etc), the Visitor Hosts (reception and sales), Education Co-ordinator (training) and Events Co-ordinator (PR, events and other fun stuff). The Membership Committee is chaired by the Membership Co-ordinator, with the Visitor Hosts reporting to the Membership Committee and both the Education Co-ordinator and Events Co-ordinator reporting to the Chapter Director.

We then have the Secretary/Treasurer who is the Finance Director and looks after all things involving money, including keeping accounts. Their job is also to assist the Chapter Director and look after the 10 Minutes speakers.

Then there is the Membership Co-ordinator who is the Marketing and HR Director and they have two key roles, building the business and ensuring that the company runs as directed. They also assist the Chapter Director as required.

Lastly, we have the Chapter Director, who is the Managing Director of the company. And like any Managing Director they are responsible for making sure that the company runs smoothly and that everyone is doing their job. They are the face of the company and provide direction and motivation.

So, depending on who is asking the question and why, I hope that helps. But, ultimately, if you want just one person, then it is the Chapter Director.

But, the final accountability rests with your Regional Director.

What do you do with mail not addressed to you?

19/11/10

Well, if you are anything like me, you either put it in the bin, leave it for someone else to open, or put it at the bottom of the pile to open later. Why? Because not much very good ever comes in a window envelope, an envelope with a label on it, an envelope where the address has been mail merged or in a manila envelope. And I bet I'm not the only one who thinks like this. You go for the nice hand-written envelopes first because we know that they are either private letters or cheques – something we want.

So, why is it that when inviting people to our Chapters by letter, some members, despite being advised of the benefits of hand writing addresses, still insist on using labels or window envelopes?

And, very often, to add insult to injury, don't even use a person's name. What's the point? It's a complete waste of time!

Often these members cite a lack of time as to why they don't follow the suggested guidelines, or just bad handwriting. Now bad writing I am just about willing to accept but, even then, I'm sure most of us can find some-one that will write a few addresses for us. Even, dare I suggest, another member of our group.

But, the excuse of no time, I'm not willing to accept. Because I tried an experiment. Even with everything I needed in my office: labels, envelopes, etc., it took me longer to load them in my printer, set up a template and print them, than it did to hand write 20 addresses on 20 envelopes. And, even if it had taken twice as long, I would still handwrite them because I know that upon receiving that envelope I would open it.

So, why do some members still avoid handwriting envelopes when they are wasting everyone's time including their own? I can think of one reason, but it's not very nice!

Leadership Teams – do you lead?

24/11/10

As a member of your Chapter's Leadership Team one of your respon-sibilities is to lead and, from time to time, it surprises me that some teams don't understand this. After all, the job description is in the title.

It can be in anything: bringing visitors, bringing referrals, getting to the Chapter early, having One2Ones, in fact everything that makes a great Chapter and earns the members more money.

And it was something I noticed again at a recent workshop. Attendance at the BNI Workshops is crucial if, as a member, we are to achieve the very best we can from our membership (I've talked about this before). A Leadership Team spends a great deal of time, along with the Events Co-ordinator, asking members to attend them and telling the members how important it is to our success. But then they don't attend themselves!

The reason I noticed the missing Leadership Team members at this particular workshop was that out of the five Chapters attending there were only Leadership Team members from one Chapter.

So, how about this for an idea?

If you are a member of a Leadership Team, ensure that at least one of you goes to every workshop in the future. It will build your credibility, give more weight to your request when asking others to attend, increase the numbers going to the workshops, and, guess what?

Increase the amount of business passed in your Chapter!

Who's in your BNI card file?

25/11/10

I'm sure that we all put into our BNI card files a few business cards of every new member that joins our Chapter, but what other cards are in there? When did you last give your file a spring clean?

The question as to whose business cards should be in your card file came up at a recent Member Success Training and my answer was easy. All the members of your Chapter.

Strangely this answer caused something of a debate because some of the more long-term BNI members present had other ideas. It seemed that their BNI card files were full of all sorts of people's business cards. So, just who should have business cards in your BNI card file? Well, the answer is very easy, as I said earlier: only the members of your Chapter and of course yours. I'll explain why.

Firstly, it is a BNI card folder, so that means only BNI members, no-one else. Secondly, only current members of your chapter: no ex-members or members of other BNI Chapters. Why? Well, again the answer is simple.

We carry our BNI card files in order to find referrals for the members of our group. Not for ex-members, members of other chapters, other business people we know or, indeed, friends. Having our business cards in each other's card file is a privilege of our membership.

Still not convinced? Well, how about looking at it like this? Say that your business card is in a fellow Chapter member's card file, but, as well as your card, there is the card of the person who was in your category before you, and the card of the member's best mate who does the same as you. How would you feel competing with two other people? Knowing that the member was recommending two other people other than you? Not impressed comes to mind.

So, why not give your BNI card file a spring clean and clear out all of those old cards. And, if you really want to keep the old cards for reference then why not get another card file – non BNI of course!

Has your Chapter already closed for Christmas?

1/12/10

It's a serious question!

Before you exclaim *"Of course not!"*, I want you to think for a minute. Just hear me out.

I was at a Chapter last week and the Leadership Team said that they wouldn't be holding their Chapter meeting on the Wednesday before Christmas, the 22nd December. And I asked whyever not? Their answer, I guess, astounded me, not so much because of their BNI meeting, but more because they are business people.

One of them said, *"I won't want to come, people will be winding down for Christmas, substitutes will be hard to find, no-one will be interested in doing business...*", the reasons just went on and on. I pointed out that, I, like many people, would be working right up until Christmas Eve, and certainly on the Wednesday, and if BNI was part of my job, there was no reason not to attend my meeting. I still want business right up until Christmas and I certainly want some in early January. Missing the 22nd December meeting would in effect be limiting any business until the middle of January!

So, my question is a serious one. Has your mind-set already closed your Chapter for Christmas?

No point looking for referrals, no point bringing visitors, members will be absent. If you have, you have already closed for Christmas.

Really successful people don't follow the herd, they do something different. So, instead of closing early for Christmas, why not make sure your business, and your BNI Chapter, are well and truly open and not only have a better December than the herd but also a great start to 2011?

Does your business card fit?

3/12/10

Pretty simple this one. I was giving my BNI business card file a spring clean and found that over 30% of my fellow member's business cards were too big to fit.

Most were too wide, some too long and others, well, just a strange size. Being different can be a good thing, but not when you want your business card in every member's card file. As members that's what we all want. Every time a member shows their card file to one of their contacts, we want our business card in it. It means the potential for referrals – more business.

So, what's the ideal size? Well, I think it is this: 86mm x 54mm. Almost credit card size. But, please do check yourself and then get your graphic designer or printer to produce a card that size.

Then, with your new cards, the perfect size, make sure that every member of your Chapter has some (and they are in their card files) and that the

Chapter business card box has a good supply as well. It's amazing the number of members that don't have their cards in the Chapter card box, when every week the Chapter director invites the visitors to take the business cards of the members.

Not having cards in member's card files or cards in the Chapter business card box are lost opportunities. Business is already tough, please don't make it harder than it need be.

Do you wear your BNI ribbons?

11/12/10

BNI ribbons – you know the ones I mean: Leadership Team, Visitor Host, Membership Committee, Education Co-ordinator, Ambassador, 7 Year Member, etc.

Well, I was making a Chapter visit recently and updating the ribbons for the years of membership of the members in the group. For one member I had a six-year ribbon and I noticed that as I approached them they didn't already have a five-year ribbon. So, I was feeling pretty good about being able to give them their ribbon. But, when I did, I was rather shocked because they said they didn't want it – they didn't wear ribbons!

I almost told them that's not an option (but I guess it is), so instead asked why. And, their answer worried me, as the benefits of wearing the year ribbon it seemed had not been explained: the member thought there was no point and that they were silly!

I guess with the Leadership Team ribbons and the others of that type their function is obvious, but I suppose with the year ribbons their purpose is not so clear.

In short, the year ribbons are all about credibility: both the member's and BNI's. Think what it says about you if you wear a 6 year ribbon. Firstly, that you have been a member of your Chapter for six years: five years running your Chapter have been happy to renew you. It also shows that you have been in business for at least six years. And, if the ribbon is attached to a blue Notable Networker badge, what does that say? All of these things help to build your credibility, your reputation. Surely no Chapter would renew your membership if you were rubbish at your job? And, what does that mean? Yes, more business!

Then there is the credibility of BNI, or, more importantly, your Chapter. When visitors come to our Chapters we want them to buy into them, to join us. So, what does it say about our Chapter if we have members who have been in the group for six years, ten years, twelve years even? It says that BNI is a serious business. That these people really believe in what they are doing, that they believe in each other. And, again, what does that mean? Yes, you've got it, more business.

So, please wear your ribbons because it just makes good business sense!

Does inviting by postcard really work?

14/12/10

It's a question that I am often asked, both by new and longer term members. And, I have to say from my own experience, yes without a doubt. Plus it can be one of the easiest ways to invite people that you will ever come across.

Last year I took twenty seven visitors along to my Chapter and a fair number of them were invited by postcard. As I say, it's one of the easiest ways to invite and I use postcards every single week. And, here's how.

All you need are two postcards. Fill them out now, with the details of your next meeting, and put them in your jacket pocket or handbag. Okay, you now have a week to use those two postcards, otherwise they will be wasted.

And, it's simple! Whenever you are out and about, it really doesn't matter where, and you get talking with someone about business and you get to *"Could you handle more?"*, no matter how much time pressure your are under, you have the answer. Give them your prepared postcard and ask them to call you. If they really are looking for more business they will call, if not, nothing has been lost, but they might just keep that card for future use. Someone turned up at our meeting once with a card that had been sent out by post six months earlier – I've still got it somewhere. If all else fails, put your card under the windscreen wiper of a trade van!

Then of course there are the 20 postcards that every new member should bring to our Chapters. How many new members do you know that have brought these in? Did you? These postcards are sent to the new member's best contacts: just imagine the results that we could get if they did!

And there are some Chapters who know just how easy postcards are to use that they design and print their own. Now I don't know if the results are any better than using those postcards supplied by BNI, but it does show how effective Chapters believe postcards to be.

So, do postcards work? Yes, as I say without a doubt. Why not try them and let me know how you get on?

Below are a couple of examples of chapter postcards I picked up a while ago. Please remember, if you would like to design your own Chapter postcard, get your design passed by your BNI Director.

Forget your BNI card file!

21/12/10

Or, should it be forgot your BNI card file? One of the most productive ways of finding referrals is to get your BNI card file into people's hands, so that they can look through it. You don't need to do anything else other than to say that the cards in the file are those of people that you know and trust and that you can highly recommend. It's also a great idea to add that you may not need their services now, but they might be of interest in the future, and that you can give them a personal introduction. You will be surprised at how often someone says, *"just what I've been looking for"* when they come across one of your fellow member's cards.

But, how do we get it into people's hands? Well, this is where forget/forgot, comes into play. How about this for an idea? You take your card file to every meeting you have and also to every job you do. And, very simply, when you leave you leave your card file behind. Now, one of two things will happen. First, someone will call you to ask if you left behind a burgundy file with gold lettering on it. You then say, *"Thank you so much, you're a life saver. That file has all of my most important contacts in. Is it okay if I collect it tomorrow?"* Obviously, they will say of course. You then add, *"As you have the file, why not take a look through it?"* and add the words above.

The second thing that can happen is that no one calls. So, you call them and say, *"I don't suppose you have fold a burgundy file with gold lettering on the front?"* When they say yes, you've guessed it, you use the words above! It's such a great way to get referrals and so simple. Have fun!

Who can I help this week?

29/12/10

I think many members find it hard to find referrals because they are trying to find referrals. We have all heard things like: *"I need to find a referral this week"*, *"I would love to get this particular member a referral"*, *"Where do you find referrals?"*, *"I'm not good at finding referrals"*. I've even said it myself!

Now I know that's not what's really meant, but I believe that some members make finding referrals harder than it need be, because they are actually looking for referrals. After all, that's what we give and hope to be given.

But, how about changing the way that we think? Instead of looking for referrals, look for people to help. Who do you know that would be helped if you recommended one of your fellow members? Referrals are all about helping people: friends and business contacts that have a problem or need something.

Most of us, I'm sure, have helped a friend whose car battery is flat, by exhausting ourselves pushing their car up and down the road to get it started! And, referrals are just the same, we are helping our friends that are in need. So, how about in future looking for people that you can help and forget about looking for referrals? Whenever you see someone with a problem or someone looking for something, just try saying *"Would you like help with that?"*

I really believe that by changing the way you think about referrals that you will see a remarkable increase in the number of referrals you find!

Ambassadors do you wear your BNI pin?

31/12/10

It's a simple thing but this is all about every member you meet, and all of your fellow Chapter members, earning more money: giving and receiving more referrals.

As an Ambassador you work with your director visiting Chapters, helping where needed, to some degree acting in the role of PR, and reporting on areas where help from your Director maybe of use.

Being an Ambassador is more effective if you are a true ambassador and by that I mean a brilliant member. Now, I know that you would not have been picked by your Director to be an Ambassador if you weren't already a great member. But my question is: could you be a better member? When you walk into a Chapter, can any member question your ability to guide them?

So, here are a few questions for you. Do you wear your BNI pin? Do you wear a clear name badge (not a business card)? Have you a blue badge? Do you read SuccessNet? Have you listened to Dr Ivan Misner's CD recently? Have you read the BNI Policy Booklet? Have you read any of the BNI books? Do you attend workshops? Do you arrive early for your meetings?

Now, the above questions are not just restricted to Ambassadors, as certainly Leadership Teams and Mentors should ask themselves the same questions. I also think that any member helping to run the Chapter should.

Why? Well, because of the benefits to themselves, and as I said earlier, every member they meet. As an Ambassador, you need to be a brilliant member. The result? You become a better member! You then help other members to become better members. The result? They are better members.

Just imagine what the effect would be in your Chapter if every person who had a role became a great member. It could result in half the members of your Chapter being great. And, what do you think the effect would be on the other members of the group? Yes – they would become better members!

So, by being a brilliant Ambassador, you can have an incredible effect on the success of every BNI member you meet.

Does what you wear suit what you do?

3/1/11

Does what you wear really matter? It is a question I wish I were asked more often because yes, it does – a great deal more than you might think.

Should it? Probably not. But then a great number of shops and designer labels would be out of business if clothes didn't matter! So yes, what you wear to your Chapter meetings and Workshops does matter.

Now I'm not suggesting that we all start wearing suits everywhere that we go, but you should be wearing what represents your business. And, if you are in the trades, that's a nice clean set of overalls, not those that you would climb around under the floor in.

Why? Because every time we meet fellow members, and visitors, we are in fact in two totally, but equally important, situations. One is obvious: we are selling ourselves. But, at the same time we are being interviewed!

So, the answer as to what you should wear is simple. Whatever you would be happy wearing either when selling or going for an interview.

Let's face it, in both of those situations we would want to look our best: washed hair, clean hands, and clothes to suit the job.

Now you might be thinking: but my fellow members know me, I've got better things to do than worry about what I look like! That may be true, but you're missing the point. You would make the effort for a sales meeting or an interview, and if you want the best from your fellow Chapter members, and please don't forget your weekly visitors and the members you don't know that you meet at workshops, they have to be given the same respect.

Every single time!

At the end of the day it's about personal branding and a great number of the things that we react to are both visual and subconscious. The question is, are you making your brand easy to refer?

It's all about confidence and the right 'buying' signs. About being comfortable.

I visited a Chapter recently and met a member who was something big in finance, he was dressed like he was going to a summer BBQ, and that didn't fit the image of someone big in finance stored in my mind.

What did it matter? He sounded good. But, in fact, it mattered a great deal! I was unsure if I would be happy to refer him. My loss, you may be thinking.

True. But, what's more important is that it was his loss. All I know is that he is something big in finance – nothing more. Short-sighted of me?

Maybe. But, competition is tough and if I can find someone that makes things easier for me, that is where I will 'buy'.

So, image is really important, make sure that yours matches what you do, and you will be helping people to refer you.

No 60 Seconds

8/1/11

At a recent Presentation Skills workshop, the trainer, having just helped the members in attendance write two new 60 Seconds, asked if anyone would like the opportunity to practise their new 60 Seconds on the group.

Not one hand went up! After a little coaxing three of the forty or so members in the room gave a 60 Seconds and knowing a couple of the members concerned, their presentations were much improved. But, the amazing thing is that this happens at many workshops: when given the chance to showcase their businesses members don't appear to want to.

On this particular evening at least half of the members in the room were new to each other, so what better way of letting these members know what they did than to be one of only three members doing a full 60 Seconds? As business people we pay a great deal of money to advertise our businesses and we also need to take advantage of every opportunity given to us. So, when you are next at a workshop and the trainer asks if you would like to give your 60 Seconds, please make sure that your hand is up first out of all those in the room and that you get the chance to let all of those there know exactly how you can help them and what you are looking for.

You may just be surprised at the result!

It's a No!

10/1/11

Something we all fear is rejection, admittedly some more than others, but in some form we all hate being rejected. After all, being rejected says something about us, doesn't it? But, every one of us has been turned down in our past and we have got over the disappointment. Again this has affected each of us in different ways; some of us have been spurred on, while others have shied away from any situations where rejection might be a possible outcome.

However, we all know of cases where someone has been rejected in one place only to be accepted in another. It is said that J K Rowling was turned down by 26 publishers before she had her first book accepted. Certainly she was not going to let being turned down stop her! And how stupid must those 26 publishers be feeling now?

Now, this might all be sounding a little deep and to have very little to do with us as BNI members.

However, it has a great deal to do with our success as a member and that of our Chapters.

One of the reasons that I am given by members for not inviting visitors is the fear of the person asked saying no. The thing about that, is that any no is not a rejection of you, it's a rejection to visiting your Chapter. So, it's not personal. Okay, it may be a rejection of something that you have recommended, but are you worried if someone doesn't go to see a film you suggest? I doubt it.

But, the bigger issue is this: if you are just frightened about getting a *"No"*, by not asking you are presenting yourself with your own *"No"*. The thing is, to get a *"Yes"*, you have to ask the question!

So, next time you hesitate to ask a question, where the answer could be no, think of JK Rowling, her millions and her 26 nos. Then invite that person and you never know you might just help your Chapter to be 40 plus strong and share in a million pounds worth of business!

Not enough business from your Chapter?

15/1/11

I suppose it's a rather silly question really, as I guess we would all like more business from our Chapters. But, what I mean is, do you get a lot less business than you had hoped for?

It's an issue that troubled Dr. Ivan Misner in the early days of BNI: he talks about the problem on the CD that we get in our new member box.

Now there are many reasons why a member might not get as much business as they had hoped for from their Chapter too many to go into here. Instead, I would like to talk about one of the most effective ways of increasing the number of referrals you get, and in fact give, from your fellow members.

The answer? One2Ones.

So, if at the moment you are getting less business from your Chapter than you would like, ask yourself this question. How many One2Ones have you had in the last three months? Less than six and you will be missing out on a great deal of business. None? Well, to be honest, I really don't know what to say...

Because every well structured One2One that you have will increase your chances of receiving great referrals. Why?

Where do I start!? An improved relationship. A better understanding of the member's business. The opportunity to explain exactly what you do. The opportunity to explain exactly what you are looking for. The opportunity to explain exactly what you don't want. The chance to find out if the member really understands what you do. The list is almost endless!

The most important fact is that every good, and I stress good, One2One you have will increase the amount of business you receive from your Chapter. So, if you are not getting the amount of business that you would like from your Chapter, don't complain, don't leave, instead book some One2Ones.

But, don't go mad! One a week is just about perfect, as you can then spend time thinking about the member and seeing what you can do for them.

Why every week?

26/2/11

Something that I am asked from time to time is why we hold our meetings every week. After all, other networking groups don't and it's a big commitment having to come weekly. Surely every other week would be better?

For some people this type of networking may be ideal, it may be all that they can manage for a number of reasons, but BNI Chapters meet weekly because we build strong relationships. We know that to get to trust someone, to know them, to like them, takes time and this can't be achieved by seeing each other sporadically. After all, would you just want to see one of your best friends every few weeks and, furthermore, not even know if they were going to turn up for a meeting that you had arranged?

BNI is all about strong relationships. Relationships that are strong enough so that we can recommend our very best contacts to fellow members. I for one would certainly not risk my reputation on someone I hardly knew.

But, how about this for an even more compelling reason?

BNI have tried and tested most things over the years and give us the very best of what they have learnt works. Recently I was listening to a CD by Ivan Misner and was interested to learn that early on BNI tried fortnightly meetings: members thought that they might be better. However, they soon changed their minds! Why? Because, they discovered that a Chapter that meet fortnightly passed 52% less referrals than a chapter that met weekly. So, if you want just one good reason for meeting weekly I don't think you need to look any further than more than double the amount of business passed in the group.

One last thing. How often when a member is absent for a week, or a Chapter is closed for a week, are twice the number of referrals passed the following week? Never – in my experience!

How well do you perform your Chapter role?

2/3/11

Every role in your Chapter, be it the Chapter Director or the Events Coordinator, is uniquely responsible for the ultimate success of the Chapter.

The Chapter Director needs to run a brilliant meeting, motivate the group, and ensure that the agenda is followed and meeting finished on time. The Membership Coordinator needs to run a strong committee, so that the polices are followed, for the benefit of all, and to plan the continued growth of the Chapter. The Secretary/Treasurer needs to keep the group in profit and organise the speakers.

Then we have the Visitor Hosts, those members that are at the Chapters bright and early, and make that vital first impression on our visitors. The committee members, who along with the Membership Coordinator, help and support the whole group. The Mentor Coordinator, and mentors, who help new members, and others, to feel welcome in the chapter and get the very best from their membership.

And, of course, the Education Coordinator who organises our education and the Events Coordination who arranges socials and gets us all to the Workshops.

Every one of those people who does a great job will help the Chapter grow and each of us in turn to earn more money.

But, have you, if you hold a role, ever thought about what happens if you do a bad job? Or, at least, not a very good one.

We talk a great deal about VCP in BNI. Visibility, credibility, profitability and assume that it is a good thing. As if by being visible, it will make us credible, and therefore profitable. But, I have news for you – it won't. Visibility isn't enough on its own. You also need to be very good.

I have two examples for you to prove my point. The first had been a member of their Chapter for some time and considered a pretty reasonable member, then they joined the Leadership Team. Every week they forgot something, so no-one had any idea what was going on. They were totally disorganised. Their referral rate dropped as members lost confidence in them.

The second member took over a role half way through a term because someone had left the Chapter. They were a long term member and were considered to be, to be honest, fairly average. But the way that they performed their role transformed how people thought about them. Their credibility soared and with it the other members' efforts to find them referrals.

So, my question to you is this. Is the way that you perform your Chapter role making you look like a credible business person? If not, you could be getting a lot less referrals than you might if it did.

154

Index

Referrals

Secretary/Treasurer

Socials

Substitutes

Testimonials